# CYBERETHICS

*Morality and Law in Cyberspace*

# CYBERETHICS

## Morality and Law in Cyberspace

**Richard A. Spinello**
*Carroll School of Management, Boston College*

## JONES AND BARTLETT PUBLISHERS

*Sudbury, Massachusetts*

BOSTON    TORONTO    LONDON    SINGAPORE

*World Headquarters*
Jones and Bartlett Publishers
40 Tall Pine Drive
Sudbury, MA 01776
978.443.5000
info@jbpub.com
www.jbpub.com

Jones and Bartlett Publishers International
Barb House, Barb Mews
London W6 7PA
UK

**Library of Congress Cataloging-in-Publication Data**
Spinello, Richard A.
    Cyberethics : morality and law in cyberspace / by Richard A. Spinello.
        p. cm.
    Includes bibliographical references and index.
    ISBN 0-7637-1269-8
    1. Internet (Computer network)—Moral and ethical aspects. 2. Computers and civilization. 3. Law and ethics. I. Title.
    TK5105.875.I57 S68 2000
    303.48'34—dc21
                                                                                    99-049918

*Production Credits*
Chief Executive Officer: Clayton Jones
Chief Operating Officer: Don Jones, Jr.
President: Tom Walker
V.P., Sales and Marketing: Tom Manning
V.P., College Editorial Director: Brian L. McKean
V.P., Managing Editor: Judith H. Hauck
Director of Design and Production: Anne Spencer
Senior Marketing Manager: Jennifer M. Jacobson
Senior Acquisitions Editor: J. Michael Stranz
Production Editor: Rebecca S. Marks
Editorial/Production Assistant: Christine Tridente
Director of Manufacturing and Inventory Control: Therese Bräuer
Cover Design: Anne Spencer
Design and Composition: Graphic World Inc.
Printing and Binding: Malloy
Cover Printing: Malloy
Cover Image: © 1999 Photodisc

Printed in the United States of America
04 03 02 01      10 9 8 7 6 5 4 3

In memory of my grandmothers,
*Guiseppa Padrevita and Olga Spinello*

# CONTENTS

# PREFACE

## ▶ The Book

The development of the Internet has been one of the most remarkable technological phenomena of the last century. In the early 1980s, the Internet was known to only a handful of scientists and academics, but it is now being regularly used by more than 100 million people, and many predict that it will revolutionize everything from the practice of medicine to education. The Internet is more than merely a communications network. It is an infrastructure, helping create a new social and economic order that is characterized by global connectivity and the decentralization of authority.

The success of the Internet would not have been possible without the recent development of the World Wide Web, which has made a wide variety of media (such as text, video, and audio) available through a user-friendly interface. The Web has ignited electronic commerce and changed the face of Internet communications. As we move into a new millennium, it is beginning to have a dominating influence on our culture and to insinuate itself into many aspects of our daily lives.

This rapid development of the Web and the entire Internet economy is not without its social costs. If it is easier to publish and spread truthful and valuable information, it is also easier to spread libel, falsehoods, and pornographic material. If it is easier to reproduce and share digitized information instantaneously, it is also easier to violate copyright protection. And if it is easier to build personal relationships with consumers, it is also easier to monitor consumers' behavior and invade their personal privacy. Thus, the Internet's vast capabilities can be misused to undermine private property and to mock our traditional sense of moral propriety.

The primary purpose of this book is to carefully review the social costs and moral problems that have been triggered by the expanded use of this communications and information network. Although some of these problems are familiar ones, many are new to the fields of computer ethics and public policy. For example, much work has been done on the topic of intellectual property, but little attention has been paid to the intricate property issues revolving around Web sites such as ownership of domain names or the acceptability of linking between Web pages. In the process of examining these issues, we identify some of the legal disputes that will most likely become paradigm cases for more complex situations yet to come.

The Internet is also a challenge to legal systems, which have had a difficult time keeping up with this borderless global technology. In the past, the Internet was an unstructured electronic terrain, a frontier with few rules and restrictions. But now that cyberspace has become a widely used forum for our economic transactions and social interactions, many argue that anarchy must yield to some type of order and that new laws must be crafted to restrict and punish asocial users. Some civil libertarians, however, steadfastly resist intrusive government intervention. "Keep your hands off our 'net" is one of their favorite slogans. But is that philosophy still tenable or is it just too romantic and antiquated for a commercialized Internet?

If we do agree that the Internet needs some type of order, the key question is how that order should be imposed or how the 'net should be governed. A framework of laws and regulation is one solution, but there are others such as greater reliance on self-regulation from below with the help of technology. Why not let technology correct itself? There are, after all, viable Internet architectures that can deal with some of the Internet's social problems, perhaps even more effectively than a centrally imposed set of regulations. These two approaches represent the fundamental options for the future of cybergovernance. Should the state, for example, promulgate and enforce laws that ban pornography, or should individual users rely on filtering devices to keep it out of their homes? *Is the proper model centralized state controls or decentralized individual controls?*

In Chapter Two, we present the case for greater reliance on a decentralized, bottoms-up approach to governing the Internet. Its proponents argue that this approach best fits the Internet's open architecture along with the logic of this medium. It can also overcome some of the administrative difficulties of controlling an international network. It is difficult for any nation to exercise local jurisdiction over the information available in cyberspace. However, it is often possible for technology itself to constrain behavior without the need for the heavy hand of government. According to this perspective, the role for government involvement in regulating the Internet should be as modest as possible. There may be externalities or market imperfections that cannot be handled by technology, such as monopolistic behavior that threatens the Internet economy. Such situations may warrant strong government intervention, but otherwise, Internet stakeholders should be allowed to govern themselves.

On the other hand, there are many perils in depending on self-regulation, especially when we empower the regulator with sound technology. There could be excesses such as the privatization of unfair copyright regulations or irresponsible content control. This has led many scholars and analysts to call for more comprehensive, top-down regulations that will ensure that the Internet is governed with regularity and fairness. Their viewpoint is also presented in Chapter Two.

Thus, the second purpose of this book is to stimulate the reader's reflection on the broad issue of Internet governance. How one resolves this fundamental question will provide an important context for addressing the formidable social problems triggered by the explosive growth of the Internet.

To accomplish both of these objectives, we first lay out some theoretical groundwork drawn from the writings of contemporary legal scholars like Larry Lessig of the Harvard Law School and philosophers like Kant and Foucault. We then focus on four broad areas: content control and free speech, intellectual property, privacy, and security. For each of these critical areas, we consider the common ethical and public policy problems that have arisen and how technology or law would propose to solve some of those problems.

The first of these four topics concerns the fringes of Internet communication, such as pornography, hate speech, and spam (unsolicited commercial e-mail). We review the history of public policy decisions about the problem of pornography and treat in some depth the suitability of automated content controls. Are these controls technically feasible, and can they be used in a way that is morally acceptable to the relevant stakeholders?

We then review the new breed of intellectual property issues provoked by the steady commercialism of the Internet and the proliferation of Web sites. These include ownership of domain names, the "right" to link to other Web sites, the propriety of framing, and the appropriate use of meta tags. We also discuss the growing reliance on trusted systems, an electronic means of ensuring that copyright protections are followed. Can these systems manage the tensions between fair use and property rights in cyberspace?

Perhaps the most notorious and widely publicized social problem is the ominous threat that the Internet poses to personal privacy. The Internet seems to have the potential to further erode our personal privacy and to make our lives as consumers and employees more transparent than ever before. What, if anything, should be done about on-line databases overflowing with personal information? The covert gathering of information from consumers visiting Web sites, the use of "cookies," and the strict monitoring of employee's Internet interactions are other problematic concerns. Here again, we explore whether certain protective technologies can be part of the solution.

Finally, we review the critical area of security with an initial focus on the perennial problem of trespass in cyberspace. We consider what constitutes trespass and why it is so odious and damaging. But the main focus of this final chapter is the use of encryption as a means of ensuring that transmitted data is confidential and secure. The encryption controversy epitomizes the struggle between government control and individual rights that is shaping many of the public policy debates about the Internet. Should users be able to encrypt data without giving the government back-door access? Or is this too big a threat to national security? In addition to a cursory overview of the federal government's policies on encryption, we analyze this matter from a moral framework to expose this dilemma to a slightly different perspective. The chapter concludes with an overview of the security issues associated with electronic commerce.

It should be apparent by now that this book is a bit more narrowly focused than traditional books about computer or information ethics, because the topics are limited to the particular moral problems that emerge in the realm of cyberspace. However, if one considers the rapid evolution of the Internet and the great potential of Web communications, what is presented here represents the new generation of moral issues that will occupy computer ethicists, lawyers, and public policy makers for many years to come.

Also, throughout the book, we implicitly embrace the philosophy of *technological realism,* which sees technology as a powerful agent for change and forward progress in society. Unlike more utopian views, this position does not ignore the dangers and deterministic tendencies of technology along with its potential to cause harm and undermine basic human rights and values.

In our view, corporations and individuals, although heavily influenced by information technology, are not yet in its thrall—they still have the capacity to control its use and curtail its injurious side effects. Such control will require prudent decision making, which will help ensure that computer technology is used wisely and cautiously, in a way that enhances the human condition and the opportunity for human flourishing. It will also demand that all information technologies, including those targeted at the social problems of cyberspace, be implemented with respect for standards of justice and fairness.

Like most traditional books on ethics, this book is optimistic about the tenacity of the human spirit and the depth of moral conviction, even in cyberspace. The technology determinists believe that the forces of technology have already won the war, but the realists contend that the struggle continues and that the final outcome is still in doubt.

## ▶ The Web Site

This book is accompanied by a Web site, www.jbpub.com/cyberethics. Although books are static entities, Web sites are dynamic and this Web site will be consistently updated and modified to reflect the changes and developments in this field. We strongly encourage both faculty and students to make ample use of this important resource.

The Web site contains valuable links to other web sites, which will facilitate further research on the topics and sub-topics covered in this book. These links also provide additional background material for some of the cases that are included at the end of each chapter. In addition, this Web site will contain elaborate exercises for each chapter, along with suggested topics for "white papers" on some of the controversial themes covered in the text. Instructors will also find sample syllabi and suggestions for organizing a course around this book and the topic of Internet ethics. Finally, the Web site will provide an opportunity for instructors and students to give the author feedback or to contact the author with questions or comments.

This book and its Web site are meant to be used jointly to enhance the academic experience of studying cyberspace ethics. One complements the other. It is our hope that both those who use this book in the classroom and the general reader will consult the Web site for its up-to-date supplementary material and its other supportive features. It is designed to make this exploration of the Internet and the ethical issues that surface there as instructive and rewarding as possible.

## ▶ Acknowledgments

In this book, I have incorporated a small amount of material from several articles or papers that I published elsewhere: a portion of the material on spam was derived from "Ethical Reflections on the Problem of Spam" originally published in *Ethics and Information Technology* (vol. 1, no. 3); several paragraphs of the discussion on James Boyle's theory of intellectual property also originally appeared in *Ethics and Information Technology* (vol. 1, no. 2); and some of the discussion on e-mail privacy rights was part of a paper titled "Electronic Mail and Panoptic Power in the Workplace," delivered at "The Fifth Annual International Conference Promoting Business Ethics" at DePaul University (October, 1998).

I am grateful to my colleagues in the Carroll School of Management at Boston College for creating an intellectual environment that is conducive to writing a book like this. A special debt of gratitude goes to the Academic Vice President's Office for its generous support of this project. I am indebted to several staff members there, especially Dr. Margaret Preston, Brendan Collins, and Aleta Mustone, for their kind assistance in helping me handle some of the mechanics involved in publishing this manuscript.

I would also like to thank a number of reviewers for their insightful and valuable advice:

Ernest Ferguson, Southwest Baptist University
Michael Bozonie, Metropolitan State University

Lawrence Daley, Hampton University
Marion Ben-Jacob, Mercy College
Kevin Treu, Furman University
Donald Gotterbarn, East Tennessee State University

Many thanks also to several individuals at Jones and Bartlett, especially Michael Stranz and Brian McKean, who believed in this project and helped push the work to its final publication in a timely fashion. Finally, I owe a great debt of gratitude to my wife, Susan T. Brinton, for her infinite supply of patience and her unflagging support. She always demonstrated remarkable tolerance for the lonely life of an author.

**Richard A. Spinello**
*September, 1999*

# CHAPTER ONE

# The Internet and Ethical Values

## ▶ Introduction

It has been more than three decades since the first communications were transmitted over a fledgling global network, which would later be called the Internet. At that time, few would have predicted the Internet's explosive growth and persistent encroachment on our personal and professional lives. From its earliest days, this radically decentralized network has put extraordinary power into the hands of individual users. For example, Internet technology has enhanced our capacity to exercise the right of free speech, and it has even given individuals the ability to protect their speech by means of encryption tools.

Many governments are clearly threatened by some of this decentralized power and have sought to impose some centralized controls on this anarchic network. The United States has attempted to regulate speech through the ill-fated Communications Decency Act and to restrict the use of encryption technology through its key recovery scheme. The 'net and its stakeholders have steadfastly resisted the imposition of such control, which has led to many of the tensions and controversies that we consider throughout this book.

Although the control of technology through law and regulation has often been a futile effort, "correcting" technology with other technology has been far more effective. The regime of law has had a hard time suppressing the dissemination of pornography on the Internet, but blocking software systems that filter out indecent material have been much more successful. This reflects the net's paradoxical nature—it empowers individuals and allows them to exercise their rights, including free speech, more vigorously, but it also makes possible effective technical controls that can undermine those rights.

Although the primary axis of discussion in this book is the ethical issues that surface on the Internet, we must devote attention to these related matters of cybergovernance and public policy. Thus, we explore in some detail the tensions between the radical empowerment that the 'net allows and this impulse to reimpose central controls.

In this introductory chapter our purpose is more modest, as we provide a concise overview of the traditional ethical frameworks that can guide our analysis of the rules and polices of cyberspace. These frameworks offer some general avenues or approaches for coming to terms with the nuanced and complex moral problems that arise on the electronic frontier.

More important, we also elaborate here on the two underlying assumptions of this work: (1) the *directive* role of moral ideals and principles in determining the regulatory landscape of cyberspace and (2) the capacity of free and responsible human beings to exercise some control over the forces of technology (technological realism).

### ▶ Cyberethics and the "Law of the Horse"

The first premise of this work may seem somewhat obvious. Surely there is a role for ethics in the control and regulation of behavior in this new region we now call cyberspace. But what is that role? How will ethics relate to the new laws of cyberspace, and how can it contend with market forces there? When we read about cyberspace regulations, scant attention is often paid to ethics. Consider, for example, Larry Lessig's highly influential essays titled "The Law of the Horse" and "The Laws of Cyberspace."[1] The axis around which these essays turn is Lessig's description of the four constraints that regulate behavior in cyberspace: law, norms, the market, and "code." This mirrors the regulations we find in real space that are also a function of these four constraints.

Laws, such as those that provide copyright and patent protection, regulate behavior by prescribing or forbidding certain activities and by imposing sanctions for violators. There is a lively debate about whether cyberspace requires a unique set of laws or whether the laws that apply to real space will apply here with some adjustments and fine tuning. Judge Frank Easterbrook, quoted in Lessig's article, has said that just as there is no need for a "law of the horse," there is no need for a "law of cyberspace."[2]

Markets too regulate behavior in various ways—advertisers gravitate to more popular Web sites, enabling those sites to enhance services; the pricing policies of the Internet service providers determine access to the

Internet; and so forth. It should be noted that the constraints of the market are often different in cyberspace than they are in real space. For example, pornography is much easier and less expensive to distribute in cyberspace than in real space, and this increases its available supply.

Software "code," that is, programs and protocols used on the Internet, also constrain and control activities. These programs are often called the *architectures of cyberspace*. Code limits access to certain Web sites by demanding a username and password. Software programs have recently appeared that effectively filter out unsolicited commercial e-mail (or spam). There are no federal laws to contain the rogue, antisocial activities of spammers, which rankle many users, but there is code to contain their efforts.

Finally, there are norms that regulate cyberspace behavior, including Internet etiquette and social customs. For instance, flaming is considered "bad form" on the Internet, and those who do it will most likely be chastised by other members of the Internet community.

However, these norms should be differentiated from fixed ethical standards. Although some of them may approximate or be based on such standards, they are, for the most part, social cultural action guides whose validity somewhat depends on custom, prevalent attitudes, public opinion, and myriad other factors.

Lessig would probably include ethical standards in the broad category he calls "norms," but in our view, cultural norms should be segregated from ethical ideals and principles. Cultural norms are relative and depend on a given social or cultural environment. Just as customs differ from country to country, the social customs of cyberspace could be quite different from the customs found in real space. Also, these customs will likely undergo some transformation over time as the Internet continues to evolve. The fundamental principles of ethics, however, are meta-norms because they have universal validity. They remain the same whether we are doing business in Venezuela or interacting in cyberspace. Like cultural norms, they are prescriptive, but unlike these norms, they have lasting and durable value because they transcend space and time.

Our assumption that ethics and customs (or cultural norms) must be kept distinct defies the popular notion of ethical relativism, which often equates the two. A full refutation of that viewpoint is beyond the scope of our discussion here. But consider the following reflection of the contemporary philosopher Phillippa Foot:

> Granted that it may be wrong to assume identity of aim between people of different cultures; nevertheless there is a great deal all men have in common. All need affection, the cooperation of others, a place in community, and help in trouble. It isn't true to suppose that human beings can flourish without these things—being isolated, despised or embattled, or without courage or hope. We are not, therefore, simply expressing values that we happen to have if we think of some moral systems as good moral systems and others as bad.[3]

None of this by any means invalidates Lessig's framework. His chief insight is that "code and market and norms and law together regulate in cyberspace as architecture and market and norms and law regulate in real space."[4] Also, according to Lessig, "Laws affect the pace of technological change, but the structures of software can do even more to curtail freedom. In the long run the shackles built by programmers could well constrain us more."[5] This notion that private code can be a more potent constraining force than public law has significant implications. The use of code as a surrogate for law may mean that certain public goods or moral values once protected by law will now be ignored or compromised by those who develop or use this code. Moreover, government itself may regulate the architectures of cyberspace to make it more controllable. Government could, for example, mandate the traceability of all Internet transactions, thereby increasing its capacity for surveillance or oversight of all interactions in cyberspace. In the hands of the private or public sector, the architectures of cyberspace can have extraordinary regulatory power.

Thus, Lessig's model is quite instructive, and we will rely on it extensively in the pages to come. However, I would argue that the model would be more useful for our purposes if greater attention were given to the role of fixed ethical values as a constraining force. But how do these values fit with the other regulatory forces?

Before we can answer this question, we must say something about the nature of those values. The notion that there are transcendent moral values grounded in our common human nature has a deep tradition in the history of philosophy. It is intuitively obvious that there are basic goods that contribute to human well-being or human flourishing. Although there are several different versions of what these goods might be, they are all strikingly similar, as one would expect. James Moor's list of core human goods includes life, happiness, and autonomy. This is similar to John Finnis' list of premoral goods: life, knowledge, play, aesthetic experience, sociability, religion, and practical reasonableness (which includes autonomy). (The works of Moor and Finnis are discussed later in this chapter.) According to Finnis, these goods allow us to lead worthwhile lives and to achieve genuine human flourishing. Hence the master principle of morality: one's choices should always be open to human fulfillment, *or* humanity, whether in oneself or in others, must be respected. None of our projects or objectives provide sufficient reason for not respecting each person's well-being, which depends on participation in these basic human goods.

Thus, the ultimate good of human flourishing should function as a prescriptive guidepost of enduring value, serving as a basis for crafting laws, developing social institutions, or regulating the Internet. Because this moral ideal is rather lofty, its application to policy making can be difficult. As a result, ethicists have proposed that we also be guided by more elab-

orate theories or by intermediate ethical principles such as nonmaleficence and justice, which are derived from the core goods but which can
function as more practical guidelines for moral decision making. We discuss one approach using such principles later in this chapter.

Therefore, we contend that these lasting moral goods essential for human flourishing should play an architectonic, or *directive role,* in the regulation of cyberspace; that is, they should guide and direct the ways in
which code, laws, the market, and social norms exercise their regulatory
power. The value of human flourishing is the ultimate constraint on our
behavior in real space and in cyberspace. Accordingly, we have enhanced
Lessig's model as depicted in Figure 1.

To illustrate our point about the role of ethics, let's consider regulations
imposed by code. There are responsible and irresponsible ways of developing code that constrains behavior. As we will see in Chapter 3, blocking software systems have become a common way of protecting young children
from pornography. Those who write this code have developed proprietary
blocking criteria, and as a rule, they do not reveal these criteria or the specific sites that are blocked. In some cases, sex education or health-related
sites are filtered out along with the pornography. If this is done inadvertently, the software should be fixed; if it is done deliberately, parents should
be informed that the scope of the filtering mechanism is broader than just
pornography. One could certainly make the case that parents should know
what the blocking criteria are to make an informed judgment about the suitability of this software. Failure to reveal this information is tantamount to
disrespecting parental autonomy. As a result, one could argue that when the
criteria are completely concealed, the code is not being deployed in a responsible manner that is consistent with the core good of autonomy.

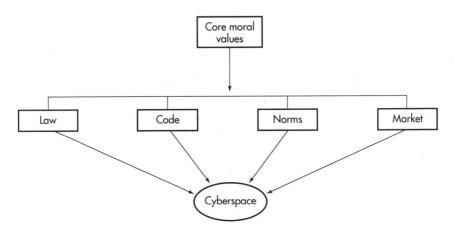

**FIGURE 1** Constraints of Cyberspace Activities (Adapted from Professor Lessig's framework.)

I am not suggesting that this is a clear-cut matter or that moral principles can provide all of the answers to proper cyberspace regulations. I also am not making a judgment about whether law or code is the more effective constraint for cyberporn. I am simply claiming that those who write these programs or formulate laws to regulate cyberspace should rely on ethics as a guide. Code writers must be responsible and prudent enough to incorporate into the new architectures of cyberspace structures that preserve basic moral values such as autonomy and privacy. Furthermore, government regulations of cyberspace must not yield to temptation to impose excessive controls. Regulators too must be guided by high moral standards and respect for basic human values such as freedom and privacy. The code itself is a powerful sovereign force, and unless it is developed and regulated appropriately, it will surely threaten the preservation of those values.

The role of morality should now be quite evident: *it must be the ultimate regulator of cyberspace that sets the boundaries for activities and policies.* It should direct and harmonize the forces of law, code, the market, and social norms so that interactions and dealings there will be measured, fair, and just.

## ▶ An Iron Cage or a Gateway to Utopia?

Although most of us agree that some constraints will need to be imposed on the technologies of networking and computing that have come to pervade the home and workplace, there is legitimate skepticism about anyone's ability to control the ultimate evolution and effects of these technologies. Are our attempts to regulate cyberspace merely a chimera? Are we too trammeled by the forces of technology or still capable of exercising sovereignty over the code that regulates cyberspace?

As we observed in the Preface, some philosophers have long regarded technology as a dark and oppressive force that menaces our individuality and authenticity. These technology determinists see technology as an independent and dehumanizing force beyond humanity's capacity to control it. The French philosopher Jacques Ellul presents a disturbing vision of technology in his seminal work *The Technological Society.* His central argument is that *technique* has become a dominant and untranscendable human value. He defines technique as *"the totality of methods rationally arrived at and having absolute efficiency* (for a given stage of development) in *every* field of human activity."[6] According to Ellul, technique is beyond our control; it has become autonomous and "fashioned an omnivorous world which obeys its own laws and which has renounced all tradition."[7] For Ellul, modern technology has irreversibly shaped the way we live, work, and interact in this world.

Ellul was not alone in advancing such a pessimistic outlook on technology. Max Weber coined the term *iron cage* to connote how technology locks us in to certain ways of being or patterns of behavior. Martin Heidegger saw technology not merely as a tool that we can manipulate but as a way of "being in the world" that deeply affects how we relate to that world. But is it really so that technology forces us into this "iron cage," and into a more fragmented, narrow-minded society dominated by the perspective that Weber labels as "instrumental reason." Before we attempt to answer this question, we must consider the other end of the spectrum, the so-called neutrality thesis about technology.

In contrast to the bleak outlook of Ellul and Heidegger, technology neutralists argue that technology is a neutral force, completely dependent on human aims and objectives. According to this viewpoint, technologies are free of bias and do not promote one type of behavior over another. Technology is only a tool, and it does not compromise our human freedom or determine our destiny in any appreciable way—it is up to us whether this powerful force is used for good or ill purposes.

Some go even further and embrace a sort of "technological utopianism," which regards certain technologies as making possible an ideal world with improved lifestyles and workplaces. This optimistic philosophy assumes that humanity can eradicate many of technology's adverse effects and manipulate this tool effectively to improve the human condition.

The philosophy of technological neutralism (or for that matter, utopianism) seems problematic for several reasons. Technology does condition our choices with certain "givens," which are virtually impossible to fully overcome. Langdon Winner describes this as a process of reverse adaptation or "the adjustment of human ends to match the character of the available means."[8]

However, in our view, it is also an exaggeration to claim that technology locks us into an iron cage. The middle ground between these extreme positions is known as technological realism, which holds that "although technology has a force of its own, it is not independent of political and social forces."[9] It acknowledges that technology has reconfigured our political and social reality and that it does influence human behavior. However, although technology is determinative to some degree of how we live and work, we still have the capacity to redirect it or to subdue it when necessary. In effect, we can still shape and dictate how certain technological innovations will be deployed and restrained, particularly when there is a conflict with the common good or core human goods. Our human freedom is undoubtedly attenuated by technology's might and its atomizing tendencies, but it is not completely effaced. We can still choose to implement systems and develop code in ways that protect fundamental human rights such as autonomy or privacy.

In this postmodern age, such a position may also seem simplistic and outdated. Although social psychologists talk about the "social construction of the self" and French psychoanalysts like Jacques Lacan refer to the unconscious as the controlling center of the self, we still presume that beneath it all is a conscious, thinking self or moral agent responsible for its actions *and* responsible for making choices about the deployment of various technologies.

Beyond any doubt, technology and its counterpart instrumental rationality are dominant forces in this society and exert enormous pressures on us to make choices and behave in certain ways. But as Charles Taylor points out, one can find throughout history pockets of concerted opposition to technology. Furthermore, the chances for such successful resistance are greatly enhanced when there is some common understanding about a particular threat or imperilment, such as the threat to our ecology that occupied us during the 1970s. Perhaps the same common consciousness will emerge about the threat to personal privacy, and this will provide yet another impetus for human choice to trump the dominating forces of information technology. Although we should not be overly optimistic about our freedom and our capacity for resisting the seductive thrall of technology, we must recognize that we still have *some* degree of freedom in this world. Thus, we agree with Taylor's assessment: "We are not, indeed, locked in. But there is a slope, an incline in things that is all too easy to slide down."[10]

How then do we avoid this fatal slide? We must consider the importance of cultivating and sustaining a moral point of view while deliberating about how to constrain behavior on the Internet through market forces, code, norms, or law.

## ▶ Ethical Frameworks and the Digital Frontier

We avoid this slide and its accompanying perils only if we conscientiously adopt the moral point of view as we evaluate technological capabilities and make decisions about the ground rules of the digital frontier. How can we characterize this moral point of view? According to Kenneth Goodpaster, it can be seen "as a mental and emotional standpoint from which all persons have a special dignity or worth, from which the Golden Rule derives its worth, and from which words like *ought* and *duty* derive their meaning."[11] This is consistent with our earlier claim that the fundamental moral imperative is the promotion of human flourishing, in both ourselves and others.

Several distinct types of ethical reasoning have been associated with the moral point of view, and they provide us with the basic principles that serve as a moral yardstick or "compass" that can assist us in making normative judgments. Our discussion here is concise, but for the interested reader, it can certainly be amplified by many other books on ethical theory or on applied ethics.[12] We consider several models of ethical reasoning based on moral frameworks, emphasizing the maximization of social utility, natural rights, contract rights, and moral duties.

The fact that several different theories embody the moral point of view does not contradict our assumption regarding the core human goods, which forms the basis of a unifying moral framework. All of these theories would recognize such goods in one form or another. Kant would embrace the principle that we must respect humanity in all of our choices and actions, although he might define "humanity" differently than Finnis. Rights-based theories discuss core human goods in terms of protection of human rights, such as the rights to life, liberty, and the pursuit of happiness. The utilitarian approach puts a great deal of emphasis on happiness and, although it may have a hard time standing on its own, it can be complemented by other theories to form a comprehensive framework.

All of these theories are worth careful consideration. Each represents a valuable perspective from which complex moral issues can be assessed and reflected upon. They help us to engage in the critical moral analysis necessitated by the thorny dilemmas that are beginning to surface all over the Internet.

Before we discuss these theories, it is worth pointing out that modern ethical frameworks fall under two broad categories: teleological or deontological. The word *teleological* is derived from the Greek term *telos,* which means goal or end. These theories argue that the rightness or wrongness of an action depends on whether they bring about the end in question (such as happiness). Deontological theories, on the other hand, consider actions to be intrinsically right or wrong—their rightness or wrongness does not depend in any way on the consequences that they effect. These frameworks emphasize duty and obligation (*deon* is the Greek word for duty).

## Utilitarianism

The philosophy of utilitarianism was developed by John Stuart Mill (1806–1873) and Jeremy Bentham (1748–1832). Utilitarianism is a teleological theory, which means that it gives priority to reaching a certain end or goal. According to this theory, the good or the end *(telos)* is happiness, or more specifically, "the greatest happiness for the greatest number of people." This good can also be described in terms of our general welfare or beneficence or even in terms of "utility." Mill refers to morality as based on the principle of utility, which he describes this way: "Actions are right in proportion as they tend to promote happiness, wrong as they tend to produce the reverse of happiness."[13]

Utilitarianism should not be confused with ethical egoism. An action is right not if it produces the most happiness for the person performing that action, but rather, it must promote the cumulative happiness for *all* parties affected by the action. Utilitarianism is the moral doctrine that we should act in order to promote the general good. According to William Frankena, this view "says that the sole ultimate standard of right, wrong, and obligation is the *principle of utility* or *beneficence,* which says quite strictly that the moral end to be sought in all that we do is *the greatest possible balance of good over evil.*"[14] Like all teleological theories, then, utilitarianism is committed to the maximization of a specific end or goal, and that end is the optimization of consequences.

On a practical level, utilitarianism requires us to make moral decisions by means of a rational, objective cost/benefit analysis. In most ethical dilemmas, one has several possible alternatives or courses of action. Once one has sorted out the most viable and sensible alternatives, each one is evaluated in terms of its costs and benefits (both direct and indirect). Based on this analysis, one chooses the alternative that produces the greatest net expectable utility, that is, the one with the greatest net benefits (or the lowest net costs) for the widest community affected by that alternative.

For example, let's assume that a corporation has to make a policy decision about inspecting its employees' e-mail messages. This might be done as a routine part of a performance review to check to make sure that workers are using e-mail only for work-related purposes and are not involved in any untoward activities. This practice is perfectly legal, but some managers wonder if it is really the right thing to do because it seems to violate the privacy rights of employees. Rightness in the utilitarian ethical model is determined by consequences that become transparent in a cost/benefit analysis. In this case, the managers might reduce their various choices to three options: (1) e-mail messages are not inspected on a routine basis and are kept confidential (unless some sort of malfeasance or criminal activity is suspected); (2) e-mail messages will be inspected regularly by managers, but employees will be informed of this policy and reminded of it every time they log in to the e-mail system so that there is no expectation of privacy; or (3) e-mail messages will be regularly but surreptitiously perused by managers with employees uninformed of the company policy. Which of these alternatives promotes the general good, that is, produces the greatest net expectable utility?

The matrix in Figure 2 will give you some idea of how this analysis might work out. It becomes clear from this exercise that it is difficult to calculate *objectively* the diffuse consequences of our actions or policies and to weight them appropriately. Herein lies a major obstacle in using this approach. Nonetheless, there is value in performing this type of analysis because it induces us to consider the broad consequences of our actions and to take into account the *human,* as well as the economic, costs of implementing various technologies.

| | Costs | Benefits |
|---|---|---|
| (1) Confidential e-mail | Lack of control over employees; difficult to prevent misuses of e-mail; e-mail could be used for various personal reasons without company knowledge. | Maintains morale and an environment of trust and respect for workers; protects personal privacy rights. |
| (2) Inspect e-mail messages with employees informed of policy | Violates privacy rights; diminishes trust and impairs morale; workers less likely to use e-mail if communications are not confidential—instead they will rely on less efficient modes of communication. | Prevents misuse along with inappropriate comments about superiors and fellow workers via e-mail; workers know the risks of using e-mail; they are less likely to use e-mail for personal purposes. |
| (3) Inspect e-mail messages surreptitiously | Same as option (2) but even more loss of trust and morale if company policy is uncovered. | Better chance to catch employees doing something wrong, such as transmitting trade secrets; perfectly legal. |

**FIGURE 2** Illustrative Cost/Benefit Analysis

Although this theory does have certain strengths, it is also seriously flawed in some ways. Depending on the context, utilitarianism could be used to justify the infliction of pain on a small number of individuals for the sake of the happiness or benefits of the majority. There are no intrinsically unjust or immoral acts for the utilitarian, and this poses a problem. What happens when human rights conflict with utility? Can those rights be suppressed on occasion for the general good? There is nothing in utilitarianism that would prevent this from happening as long as a cogent and objective case is made that the benefits of doing so exceeds the costs. The primary problem then is that this theory lacks the proper sensitivity to the vital ideals of justice and human rights.

## Contract Rights (Contractarianism)

Another mode of reasoning that exemplifies the moral point of view is rights-based analysis, which is sometimes called *contractarianism*. It looks at moral issues from the viewpoint of the human rights that may be at stake. A "right" is simply an entitlement or a claim to something. For example, thanks to the Fourth Amendment, American citizens are entitled to protection from unwarranted search and seizures in the privacy of their homes. In contrast to the utilitarian view, the consequences of an action are morally irrelevant for those who support contractarianism. Rights are unequivocally enjoyed by all citizens, and the rights of the minority cannot be suspended or abolished even if that abolition will maximize the welfare of the majority.

An important distinction needs to be made between positive and negative rights. Possession of a negative right implies that one is free from external interference in one's affairs. Examples of negative rights include the right to free speech, the right to property, and the right to privacy. Because all citizens have a right to privacy in their homes, the state cannot interfere in their affairs by tapping their phone calls unless it has demonstrated a strong probability that laws are being broken.

A positive right, on the other hand, implies a requirement that the holder of this right be provided with whatever one needs to pursue one's legitimate interests. The rights to medical care and education are examples of positive rights. In the United States, the right to universal health care is rather dubious but the right to education is unequivocal. Therefore, the state has a duty to educate children through the twelfth grade. If everyone had a "right" to Internet access, there would be a correlative duty on the part of the government to provide that access for those who could not afford it.

Rights can be philosophically grounded in several ways. Some traditional philosophers, such as Locke and Rousseau, and the contemporary social philosopher John Rawls claim that we have basic rights by virtue of an implicit social contract between the individual and civil society. Individuals agree to a contract outside of the organized civil society, which stipulates the fundamental principles of their association, including their rights and duties. Rights are one side of a quid pro quo—we are guaranteed certain rights (for example, life, liberty, and the pursuit of happiness) as long as we obey the laws and regulations of civil society. This contract is not real according to Charles Kelbley because "we are not discussing facts but an ideal which rational individuals can embrace as a standard to measure the moral nature of social institutions and efforts at reform."[15]

According to this perspective, moral reasoning should be governed by respect for these individual rights and by a philosophy of fairness. As Ken Goodpaster observes, "fairness is explained as a condition that prevails when all individuals are accorded equal respect as participants in social arrangements."[16] In short, this rights-based approach to ethics focuses on the need to respect an individual's legal, moral, and contractual rights as the basis of justice and fairness.

The problem with most rights-based theories is that they do not provide adequate criteria for resolving practical disputes when rights are in conflict. For example, those who send spam (unsolicited commercial e-mail) over the Internet claim that they are exercising their right to free speech, but many recipients argue that spam is intrusive and is therefore an invasion of their right to privacy. The real difficulty is how we adjudicate which right takes priority, and rights-based theories are not always helpful in making this determination.

## Natural Rights

One wonders how firm the ground is beneath this social contract. Is there some other way to legitimate basic human rights that is not contingent on such a contract? The tradition of natural law philosophy supposes that all human beings have fundamental natural rights that are grounded in their common human nature. It stresses that human fulfillment or human flourishing is the final goal of existence—one's ultimate purpose in life is to realize his or her potential as a human person to the fullest extent possible. Hence, it allows us to evaluate information management practices and policies from a unique vantage point: do those policies and practices adequately respect and foster human well-being and contribute to or impede human flourishing?

John Finnis, a contemporary natural law philosopher, has attempted to develop an updated natural law ethic that remains faithful to the broad lines of natural law theory as developed in the philosophy of St. Thomas Aquinas. Recall his claim that there are seven irreducible premoral goods that are the key to our flourishing as humans: (1) life and health, (2) knowledge, (3) play, (4) aesthetic experience, (5) sociability (or friendship), (6) religion, and (7) practical reasonableness. Practical reasonableness, which includes the value of autonomy, is the most important of these because it shapes one's participation in the other basic goods. And one requirement of practical reasonableness is that it is unreasonable to choose directly against any basic value, "whether in oneself or in one's fellow human beings."[17] Furthermore, a corollary of this duty are clear human rights—for example, the right to life, the right to the truth in factual communications, the right not to be condemned on false charges, and so forth.[18]

The natural law/natural rights tradition has been neglected in most books on business and computer ethics perhaps because of its presumed impracticality. However, it does provide us with a valuable vantage point to judge ethical conundrums in cyberspace. It compels us to consider whether certain policies or actions are consistent with human flourishing, that is, with the realization of core human goods identified by Finnis. Or do they contradict the rights that flow from the overarching duty not to choose deliberately against any basic human value? If these questions cannot be answered satisfactorily, it is surely a sign that something is seriously wrong.

Although Finnis has tried to disengage his natural rights framework from the cumbersome metaphysics of Aquinas, his critics claim that he does not succeed. They contend that his list of premoral goods is arbitrary and that for natural law to work, an underlying ontology is essential. According to this critique, it is unclear how Finnis justifies his list of the basic forms of the good. Finnis contends that they are basic goods that reasonable persons would accept upon serious reflection. According to Anthony Lisska, however, "One intuits the basic goods and it just happens that set of goods correspond to human well being. But what establishes the causal relationship?"[19] This is obviously a complicated issue which cannot be further explored, but it is worth pointing out that Finnis does offer a substantial rationale for each of these goods, and this contributes to the objectivity and plausibility of his position.

## Moral Duty (Pluralism)

The final framework is based on the moral philosophy of Immanuel Kant (1724–1804), which can be found in his short but difficult masterpiece on ethics *Fundamental Principles of the Metaphysics of Morals*. It assumes that the moral point of view is best expressed by discerning and carrying out one's moral duty. This duty-based, deontological ethical framework is sometimes called *pluralism.*

Kant believed that consequences of an action are morally irrelevant: "an action performed from duty does not have its moral worth in the purpose which is to be achieved through it but in the maxim by which it is determined."[20] According to Kant, actions have moral worth only when they are done for the sake of duty. But what is our duty, and how is it derived? In Kant's systematic philosophy, our moral duty is simple: to follow the moral law, which like the laws of science or physics, must be rational. Also, like all rational laws, the moral law must be universal because universality represents the common character of rationality and law. This universal moral law is expressed as the categorical imperative: "I should never act except in such a way that I can also will that my maxim should become a universal law."[21] The imperative is "categorical" because it does not allow for any exceptions.

A "maxim," as referred to in Kant's categorical imperative, is an implied principle or rule underlying a particular action. For example, if I usually break my promises, then I act according to the private maxim that promise breaking is morally acceptable when it is in my best interests to do so. But can one take this maxim and transform it into a universal moral law? As a universal law, this particular maxim would be expressed as follows: "It is permissible for everyone to break promises when it is in his or her best interests to do so." Such a law, however, is invalid because it entails a logical contradiction. Universal promise breaking is logically impossible (like a square circle) because if everyone broke promises, the whole idea of promising would lose its intelligibility. A "promise" would not exist because in such a climate, anyone making a promise would lack credibility. Thus, this maxim is clearly contradictory, and it would destroy itself as soon as it was transformed into a universal law. According to Kant, then, any self-contradictory universalized maxims such as this one are morally forbidden.

Kant's categorical imperative is his ultimate ethical principle. It is the acid test of whether an action is right or wrong. Actions that cannot pass the test of universalization are prohibited. The categorical imperative functions as a guide, a "moral compass," that gives us a reliable way of determining a correct and consistent course of action. According to Norman Bowie, "the test of the categorical imperative becomes a principle of fair play—one of the essential features of fair play is that one should not make an exception of oneself."[22]

Also, from the categorical imperative we can derive other duties such as the duty to keep contracts, to tell the truth, and to avoid injury to others. Kant would maintain that each of these duties is also categorical, admitting of no exceptions, because the maxim underlying such an exception cannot be universalized.

How might we apply Kant's theory to the rather mundane ethical dilemmas that arise in cyberspace? Let's return once again to the problem of spam. Spamming clearly violates the spirit of Kant's categorical imperative, which requires us to perform only those actions that can be universalized. In this case, we must imagine what would happen if all organizations and vendors that had an interest in on-line advertising adopted a policy of spamming, that is, regularly transmitting volumes of bulk e-mail through cyberspace. Beyond any doubt, the global e-mail system and even the Internet itself would rapidly become dysfunctional. Spamming then is not a coherently universalizable practice.

At the heart of Kant's ethical system is the notion that there are rational constraints on what we can do. We may want to engage in some action (such as sending millions of unsolicited e-mail messages), but we are inconsistent and hence unethical unless we accept the implications of everyone doing the same thing. According to Kant, it is unethical to make arbitrary exceptions for ourselves, which is exactly what the spammers are *implicitly* doing. In the simplest terms, the categorical imperative suggests the following question: what if everybody did what you are doing? In this case, if everybody practiced spamming, the result would be a calamity for the Internet.

Before concluding this discussion on Kant, it is worth citing his second formulation of the categorical imperative: "Act in such a way that you treat humanity, whether in your own person or in the person of another, always at the same time as an end and never simply as a means."[23] For Kant, as well as for other moralists (such as Finnis), the principle of humanity as an end-in-itself serves as a limiting condition of every person's freedom of action. We cannot exploit other human beings and treat them exclusively as a means to our ends or purposes. One's projects or objectives cannot supersede the worth of other human beings. This principle can also be summed up in the notion of *respect*. One way to express universal morality is in terms of the general principle of respect for other human beings, who deserve that respect because they are free and rational persons.

One of the problems with Kant's moral philosophy is its rigidity. There are no exceptions to the moral laws derived from the absolute categorical imperative. Hence, lying is *always* wrong even though we can envision times when telling a lie is a reasonable and proper course of action (for example, to save a human life). In cases like this, there is a conflict of moral laws: the law to tell the truth and the law to save a life in jeopardy, and we have no alternative but to admit an exception to one of them. As A. C. Ewing points out,

> . . . in cases where two laws conflict it is hard to see how we can rationally decide between them except by considering the goodness or badness of the consequences. However important it is to tell the truth and however evil to lie, there are surely cases where much greater evils can still be averted by a lie, and is lying wrong then?[24]

Ewing's argument that it is difficult to avoid an appeal to consequences when two laws conflict poses problems for Kant's moral philosophy, despite its relevance for many areas of applied ethics.

William D. Ross (1877–1940), a contemporary English philosopher, proposed an alternative duty-based philosophy that attempts to obviate the difficulties posed by Kant's inflexibility. Ross argues in his book *The Right and the Good* that we are obliged to follow several basic *prima facie* duties, which each of us can intuit through simple reflection. These duties are *prima facie* in the sense that they are conditional and not absolute. This means that under normal circumstances, we must follow a particular duty, but in those unusual situations when duties conflict with one another, one duty may be overridden by another duty that is judged to be superior, at least under these specific circumstances. According to Ross, moral rules or principles are not categorical as they are for Kant, so they can have exceptions. Thus, a moral principle can be sacrificed or overridden, but only for another moral principle, not just for arbitrary, selfish, or even utilitarian reasons.

According to Ross, the seven *prima facie* moral duties that are binding on all moral agents are the following:

1. One ought to keep promises and tell the truth (*fidelity*).
2. One ought to right the wrongs that one has inflicted on others (*reparation*).
3. One ought to distribute goods justly (*justice*).
4. One ought to improve the lot of others with respect to virtue, intelligence, and happiness (*beneficence*).
5. One ought to improve oneself with respect to virtue and intelligence (*self-improvement*).
6. One ought to exhibit gratitude when appropriate (*gratitude*).
7. One ought to avoid injury to others (*noninjury*).

The Achilles' heel of Ross's theory is twofold: (1) his list of duties seems arbitrary because it is not metaphysically or even philosophically grounded; (2) the list also seems incomplete—where, for example, is the duty not to steal property from another? It may be included in number seven but that is not altogether clear. Moreover, is it really true that all human beings (even those in different cultures) simply "intuit" these same principles? Finally, *The Right and the Good* provides little help for resolving situations in which two *prima facie* duties do conflict. Ross offers few concrete criteria for determining when one obligation is more stringent and compelling than another.

Despite these shortcomings, however, Ross's framework, like the others we have considered, is not without some merit. A focus on one's moral duty (or even conflicting duties) in a particular situation is a worthy starting point for moral reasoning about some dilemma or quandary. Furthermore, for many moral conundrums, a sincere and rational person can develop sound, objective reasons for determining which duty should take priority.

## Postscript on Moral Theory

As we have seen, none of these theories are without flaws or contradictions, but they do represent viable avenues for reasoning about moral issues, especially when those issues go beyond the level of moral common sense. They also have certain elements in common, particularly an orientation to "the other"—the need to consider the stakes of various constituencies in assessing alternative action plans, the other's moral and legal rights, and our duty to treat the other as an end and not as a means. Moreover, all of these theories suggest that the worth of individual or corporate projects does not take precedence over the worth of human rights, needs, and aspirations.

Before concluding this material on ethical theory, we can summarize how they can be applied to some of the moral quandaries that arise in the electronic frontier of cyberspace. The following matrix provides a concise framework for putting these three basic theories into action:

| Theory Type | Operative Questions |
|---|---|
| Consequentialism/utilitarianism | Which action or policy generates the best overall consequences or the greatest net expectable utility for all affected parties? |
| Duty-based morality | Can the maxim underlying the course of action being considered be universalized? Is the principle of fair play being violated? If there appear to be conflicting duties, which is the stronger duty? |
| Rights-based morality | Which action or policy best protects the human and legal rights of the individuals involved? Does the proposed action or policy impede the basic requirements of human flourishing? |

In some cases, these three frameworks will converge on the same solution to an ethical quandary. At other times, they will suggest different solutions to the problem and one must decide which framework should "trump," or override, the others. This will require careful and objective reasoning, but responsible behavior will sometimes require that this extra step be taken. To be sure, the Internet will present unique ethical challenges that could never have been envisioned by Kant or Mill, but these frameworks still provide a general way of coming to terms with these tough questions.

Because each of these theories has certain shortcomings, some attempts have been made to combine the central elements of two or more frameworks. One such attempt is James Moor's model of just consequentialism. Moor, recognizing the deficiencies of pure consequentialism, argues that it must be constrained by considerations of justice. The starting point for moral reasoning is the principle of justice, the protection of human rights, including life, happiness, and autonomy. Sometimes we must interfere with those rights, but how do we determine when that is required? Moor refers us to Bernard Gert's book *Morality*, which "provides us with a notion of moral impartiality that offers a good approach to justice that is useful in resolving these conflicts."[25] Justice demands impartiality, so it is unjust for someone to adopt a policy that he or she would not allow others to adopt. Moor uses the example of adopting a policy of installing defective computer chips. If the general policy is that any company can manufacture defective goods that could be harmful to people, no rational person would accept such a policy because he or she would put himself or herself at risk.

Gert's test of impartiality involves two steps: (1) determine the applicable moral rule in a given situation; (2) consider whether that rule should be publicly allowed, i.e., what would be the consequences if everybody followed this rule? Gert refers to this impartiality as the "blindfold of justice," which does not remove general knowledge of consequences, but it does remove knowledge of who will benefit and who will be hurt by one's choices. This blindfold of justice or impartiality test is the constraint on consequentalism. If this test is applied to computing policies, "some policies will be regarded as unjust by all rational, impartial people, some policies will be regarded as just by all rational, impartial people, and some will be in dispute."

Once we have subjected a policy to the impartiality test and have determined that it is not unjust, we can then determine which of the just policies (or perhaps those in dispute) optimizes the consequences. For example, if we are considering two policies designed to promote privacy on the Internet that are both just, we should choose the one with the best outcome where the benefits most clearly outweigh the costs.

Just consequentalism, therefore, has some distinct advantages. It enables us to analyze moral dilemmas through the lens of consequences but with adequate attention given to issues of justice and human rights, which cannot be sacrificed even for the sake of maximizing the beneficial consequences for the majority.

## ▶ Normative Principles

For those who find theory too abstract to apply to complex dilemmas, another approach, which has become known as principilism, is available. It is commonly used in biomedical ethics and has become popularized through the work of Beauchamp and Childress.[27] These intermediate principles are derived from and compatible with all of the theories articulated here. They constitute *prima facie* duties that are always in force but may occasionally conflict. The four principles proposed by Beauchamp and Childress are autonomy, nonmaleficence, beneficence, and justice. Those who advocate this approach also prescribe certain "prudential requirements" that determine when one *prima facie* principle should be given more weight than another. These include "being sure that there is a realistic prospect of achieving the moral objective one has chosen to honor; no alternative course of action is possible that would honor both conflicting obligations; and we minimize the effects of infringing on the *prima facie* duty."[28]

### The Principle of Autonomy

Kant and other philosophers have consistently argued that a defining element of personhood is one's capacity to be autonomous or self-determining. According to Gary Doppelt, "the Kantian conception of personhood ties the moral identity of persons to the supreme value of their rational capacities for normative self-determination."[29] All rational persons have two key moral powers or capacities: (1) they possess the ability to develop and revise a rational plan to pursue their conception of the good life and (2) they also possess the capacity to respect this same capacity of self-determination in others. Thus, autonomy is not only a necessary condition of moral responsibility, it is also through the exercise of autonomy that individuals shape their destiny according to their notion of the best sort of life worth living. When someone is deprived of their autonomy, their plans are interfered with and they are not treated with the respect that they deserve. Of course, respect for autonomy must be balanced against other moral considerations and claims.

### The Principle of Nonmaleficence

The principle of nonmaleficence can best be summarized in the moral injunction "above all, do no harm." According to this core principle, one ought to avoid unnecessary harm or injury to others whenever possible. This negative injunction against doing injury to others is sometimes called the *moral minimum*. However one may choose to develop a moral code of conduct, this injunction must be given a pre-eminent status. Most moral systems go well beyond this minimum requirement, as we have seen in the theories already discussed, but that does not detract from the central importance of this principle. According to Jon Gunneman and his co-authors,

> We know of no societies, from the literature of anthropology or comparative ethics, whose moral codes do not contain some injunction against harming others. The specific notion of *harm* or *social injury* may vary, as well as the mode of correction and restitution but the injunctions are present.[30]

## Beneficence

Beneficence is a positive duty that has been formulated in many ways. In the simplest terms, beneficence means that we should act in such a way that we advance the welfare of other people when we are able to do so. In other words, we have a duty to help others. But what does this really mean? When am I duty bound to help another person or even an institution? It is obvious that we cannot help everyone or intervene in every situation when someone is in need. Therefore, some criteria are necessary for determining when such a moral obligation arises. In general, it can be argued that we have a duty to help others under the following conditions:

- The need is serious or urgent.

- We have knowledge or awareness of the situation.

- We have the capability to provide assistance ("ought assumes can" is the operative principle).

If, for example, one is an Olympic swimmer and sees someone drowning at the beach, one has an obligation to attempt a rescue of that person, especially if this is the only recourse and there is little risk to one's own life. This principle has some relevance when we evaluate society's questionable duty of beneficence to provide universal Internet service.

## Justice

Although theories of justice have their differences, most have in common adherence to this basic formal principle: "Similar cases ought to be treated in similar ways." Above all else, justice requires fair treatment and impartiality. This is a formal principle of justice and needs to be supplemented by the criteria for determining "similar" cases. This leads into theories of distributive justice, which attempt to formulate an underlying principle for how we should allocate society's scarce resources. Some theories emphasize equality, that is, all goods should be distributed equally. John Rawls, for example, adopts an egalitarian approach, although he argues that an unequal distribution of goods is acceptable when it works for the advantage of everyone, especially the least advantaged (the difference principle).[31] Other theories emphasize contribution and effort as formulated in this maxim: benefits or resources should be distributed according to the contribution each individual makes to the furtherance of society's goals. Still another theory of justice, which has typically been associated with socialism, argues for justice based on need: "From each according to his ability, to each according to his needs."[32]

Our purpose here is not to defend one of these theories against the other but to illustrate that moral judgments should be based in part on the formal principle of justice and should take into account some standard regarding how the benefits and burdens should be fairly distributed within a group or society at large.

There is no reason that these intermediate moral principles cannot be applied to some of the controversial problems that we consider in this book. They are certainly general enough to have applicability in the field of computer and Internet ethics as well as in the field of bioethics. A person who makes choices and develops policies attentive to these practical principles would surely be acting with the care and prudence that is consistent with the moral point of view.

## Discussion Questions

1. What is the basic difference between teleological and deontological ethical theories?
2. Explain and critically analyze the essential elements of Kant's moral system.
3. Is it possible to eliminate the consideration of consequences in the moral reasoning process?
4. Explain and critique the theory of just consequentialism.

## References

1. Lessig, L. *The law of the horse* and *The laws of cyberspace*. Available at http://cyber.harvard.edu/lessig.html.
2. Easerbrook, F. 1996. Cyberspace and the law of the horse. *University of Chicago Law Forum* 207.
3. Foot, P. 1979. *Moral relativism*. Lindley Lecture, Department of Philosophy, University of Kansas.
4. Lessig, L. *The laws of cyberspace*, p. 5.
5. Lessig, L. 1997.Tyranny in the infrastructure. *Wired* 5.07:96.
6. Ellul, J. 1964. *The technological society*. Trans. John Wilkinson. New York: Vintage Books, p. xxv.
7. Ellul, J. p. 14.

8. Winner, L. 1977. *Autonomous technology: Technics-out-of-control as a theme of political thought.* Cambridge: MIT Press, p. 229.

9. Regan, P. 1995. *Legislating privacy.* Chapel Hill, NC: University of North Carolina Press, p. 12.

10. Taylor, C. 1991. *The ethics of authenticity.* Cambridge, MA: Harvard University Press, p. 101.

11. Goodpaster, K. 1985. Some avenues for ethical analysis in management. In Matthews, J., et al. *Policies and persons.* New York: McGraw-Hill, p. 495.

12. See, for example, Chapter 2 of Spinello, R. A. 1995. *Ethical aspects of information technology.* Englewood Cliffs, NJ: Prentice Hall; Rachels, J. 1986. *The elements of moral philosophy.* New York: Random House; and Frankena, W. K. 1963. *Ethics.* Englewood Cliffs, NJ: Prentice Hall.

13. Mill, J. S. 1976. *Utilitarianism.* In Glickman, J. *Moral philosophy.* New York: St. Martin's Press, p. 540.

14. Frankena, W. K. p. 29.

15. Kelbley, C. 1975. Freedom from the good. In Johann, R. *Freedom and value.* New York: Fordham University Press, p. 173.

16. Goodpaster, K. p. 497.

17. Finnis, J. 1980. *Natural law and natural rights.* New York: Oxford University Press, p. 225

18. Finnis, J. p. 225.

19. Lisska, A. 1996. *Aquinas' theory of natural law.* New York: Oxford University Press, p. 161.

20. Kant, I. 1959. *Foundations of the metaphysics of morals.* Indianapolis: Bobbs Merrill, p. 16.

21. Kant, I. p. 18.

22. Bowie, N. 1999. *Business ethics: A Kantian perspective.* Oxford: Blackwell Publishers, p. 17.

23. Kant, I. p. 36.

24. Ewing, A. C. 1965. *Ethics.* New York: Free Press, p. 58.

25. Moor, J. 1998. *Just consequentialism and computing.* CEPE 1998 Proceedings. London: London School of Economics, p. 3.

26. Moor, J. p. 4.

27. Beauchamp, T., and Childress, J. F. 1994. *Principles of biomedical ethics,* 4th ed. New York: Oxford University Press.

28. Kaczeski, M. 1998. Casuistry and the four principles approach. In Chadwick, R. *Encyclopedia of applied ethics,* vol. 1. San Diego: Academic Press, p. 430.

29. Doppelt, G. 1988. Beyond liberalism and communitarianism: A critical theory of social justice. *Philosophy and Social Criticism* 14(3/4):278.

30. Gunneman, J., et al. 1972. *The ethical investor.* New Haven: Yale University Press, p. 20.

31. Rawls, J. 1971. *A theory of justice.* Cambridge, MA: Harvard University Press, pp. 85–90.

32. Marx, K. 1938. *Critique of the Gotha Program.* London: Lawrence and Werhart, p. 14.

# CHAPTER TWO

# Governing and Regulating the Internet

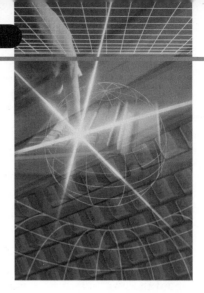

## ▶ Introduction

Although much has been written about the perils of overexposing children and teenagers to the Internet, a recent headline in *The New York Times* sounded especially ominous: "A Seductive Drug Culture Flourishes on the Internet." The article explained how the Internet is now rife with Web sites that endorse illegal drugs or provide explicit instructions for making, growing, and consuming such drugs. Many of these Web sites make drugs sound exciting and alluring and never even hint about the risks of addiction. The problem is compounded because "the Internet lacks a quality control mechanism to separate fact from hyperbole or from outright falsehood, even in discussions that may ultimately encourage an activity that remains illegal for Americans of all ages."[1]

This is a disturbing, but certainly not a surprising, development, and for some, it does not augur well for the future of this pervasive technology. But from its earliest origins, a free-wheeling spirit has dominated the rules of discourse in cyberspace. According to Jonathan Katz, "it is the freest community in America."[2] Hence, one of the most formidable issues faced by public policy makers throughout the world is whether to impose some limits on this free and unencumbered flow of information in cyberspace—to restrict, for example, the dissemination of hard core pornography or perhaps to ban or control these nefarious Web sites that promote illicit drug use. Even if a decision were made to do so, implementation of that decision would be challenging given the Internet's complexity and vast global reach.

The debate about pornography on the Internet or about Web sites advocating illicit activities reflects deeper questions about how the Internet should be regulated or governed. Although the Internet's anarchy and lack of structure has led to some excesses, many users are loath to see it replaced by tighter, centralized controls. Most civil libertarians, for example, contend that the Internet thrives precisely because there is no central governing authority. Consequently, they favor the continuation of decentralization and self-governance instead of any form of government intervention, believing that traditional forms of regulation would interfere with electronic interactions and the free flow of ideas. They argue that the Internet should be able to develop its own unique political structure, set appropriate standards, and even handle its own disputes.

However, some commercial interests on the Internet are less sanguine about the possibility that this would work effectively enough. They are more apt to favor moderate central controls as long as they do not impede electronic commerce (e-commerce). They recognize the need for some sort of rule-making authority to ensure an adequate public order in cyberspace. Chaos is usually not conducive to an attractive business environment.

For some businesses, this confusion and anarchy can expose them to legal land mines and potentially costly liabilities. Take the case of the Blue Note jazz club in Greenwich Village versus the Blue Note nightclub in Missouri. Although the Blue Note club in New York has a federal trademark for its name, the Blue Note in Missouri obtained "the right to use the trade name locally in Missouri—what is known in trademark law as a "geographical carve-out."' However, when this Blue Note designed its own Web page, the Blue Note in New York protested, claiming that its trademark had been violated by the Missouri club's worldwide presence on the Internet. As a result of this and similar cases, the legal system is still trying to decide whether business on the Internet "falls under the laws of some, all, or any of the jurisdictions from which that Internet site can be reached."[3]

Can the Internet and e-commerce really continue to thrive without more oversight and coordination? Can antisocial users and reckless cyberpunks be contained sufficiently without the firm rule of law? Will "code" inevitably impose more stringent controls than law? Or are central, hierarchical controls necessary to create a more orderly and fair environment?

Before plunging into a discussion of these complex matters, it is instructive to review the history and technology of the Internet. It is important to understand the architectures of the Internet to appreciate the various possibilities for cybergovernance. This overview includes a cursory treatment of the World Wide Web and the recent surge in e-commerce along with some of its attendant social problems. It is also instructive at this point to consider the Internet's primary stakeholders who have a substantial interest in this topic.

Our primary purpose in this chapter, however, is to discuss governance and jurisdictional issues that have significant ethical implications. We present the most prominent governance models and consider the viability of a more bottoms-up approach to regulation. No matter which combination of forces is chosen, Internet stakeholders, including the state, must behave prudently in cyberspace with due respect for the core human goods of liberty, free speech, and privacy. This will help ensure that any collateral damage that often accompanies regulatory activities will be kept to the barest minimum.

## ▶ The Internet: A Short History

For some, the *Internet* has become synonymous with the ubiquitous *World Wide Web*, but it is much more than that. In the simplest terms, the Internet is a location where multiple forms of data interconnections take place, including those involving the Web.

The origin of the Internet can be traced back to the ARPANET project of the Advanced Research Projects Agency (ARPA), a research agency of the Defense Department. In 1969, this agency provided grants to universities and corporations to develop a reliable digital communications network. This was an experimental project that investigated the optimal way of building a network that could function as a reliable communications medium, especially in time of a national emergency. This network was a great success, and it was quickly used to link together a number of researchers at remote sites. At the time, only hard-core computer scientists knew of this network's existence.

In the early 1980s, this system was subdivided into two networks: the ARPANET and Milnet. Furthermore, connections were developed so that users could communicate between the two networks. The interaction between these networks came to be known as the *Internet*. In the late 1980s, the National Science Foundation network (NSFNET), which relied on five supercomputers to link university and government researchers from across the world, replaced the ARPANET. The NSFNET began to encompass many other lower-level networks such as those developed by academic institutions, and gradually, the Internet as we know it today, a maze of interconnected networks, was born.

In these early days, the federal government generously subsidized the Internet, and as a consequence, restrictions were placed on any commercial use. The Internet was the exclusive domain of government researchers, scientists, university professors, and others who used it primarily to share their research findings or other academic information.

But the NSF no longer subsidizes the Internet, which has assumed a commercial character within the last few years. During the early 1990s, the Internet quickly became available to corporate users, and e-mail providers, such as MCI and CompuServe, opened up e-mail gateways. By 1993, 29% of the host computers connected to the Internet belonged to corporations. Commercial use now accounts for almost 60% of all Internet traffic.

The global diffusion of Internet use during this period has been an extraordinary phenomenon. In 1983, a mere 500 computers were connected to the Internet, but by 1998, more than 16 million registered host computers were connected. It has now become a vast global "network of networks," connecting millions of users in more than 60 countries. Although the rapid development of the global Internet has been extraordinary, there is still a disparity between developed and developing countries. Fortunately, some developing countries like India are investing heavily to close this gap by building up their Internet infrastructures. The government of India, for example, is attempting to link India's rural population, hoping to boost Internet connections from their present level of 250,000 to 5 million within the next five years.[4]

This global connectivity provided by the Internet is perhaps its most attractive feature. It brings together millions of people and thousands of organizations all over the world, and it has helped achieve what *The Economist* calls "the death of distance," that is, the overcoming of geographic proximity as a barrier for conducting business.

How does this all work? There is actually little physical substance to the Internet. There are a few dedicated computers at key connection junctures, but "like a parasite, the Internet uses the multi-billion dollar telephone network as its hosts and lets them carry most of the cost."[5] Data is transferred by means of a network technology called *TCP/IP*. The TCP/IP protocol allows for complete interoperability on the Internet so that computers can communicate with one another even if they have different operating systems or applications software. Therefore, TCP/IP makes the network virtually transparent to end users no matter what system they are using, and it allows the Internet to function as a single, unified network.

TCP/IP consist of two pieces. The first piece is the IP, or Internet protocol, which establishes a unique numeric address (four numbers, ranging from 0 to 255, separated by decimal points) for each system connected to the Internet. IP is a means of labeling data so that it can be sent to the proper destination in the most efficient way possible. The second piece, TCP, or transmission control protocol, enables network communication over the Internet. The data are broken up into pieces called *packets*, with the first part of each packet containing the address where it should go. The packets are then sent by a "router," that is, a server on the Internet that keeps track of Internet addresses. Packets may be sent through several different computers until they reach their ultimate destination. Once all of the packets arrive, the message or data will be reconstructed based on the sequence numbers in the headers to each packet.

The Internet's current architecture makes possible some distinctive features that have some relevance for cybergovernance. To begin with, the Internet is *asynchronous*—unlike telephone communication, there is no need for coordination between the sender and recipient of a message. An e-mail message, for example, can be sent to a mailbox that can be accessed at any time by its owner. Second, the Internet permits a *many-to-many format of communications*[6]: many users can interact with many other users through e-mail, bulletin boards, Web sites, and other vehicles. Unlike traditional media such as newspapers, the Internet is interactive because users can speak back. Third, the Internet is a *distributed* network, relying on packet-based technology. As we have seen, it is a naturally decentralized environment. There is no center to the Internet; that is, there is no central server or single controlling authority, and information can travel from one location to another without being transmitted through a central hub. This gives users more control over the flow of information. Also, because it is a packet-based network, it is more difficult to censor that information. Finally, the Internet is highly *scalable;* that is, it is not directly affected when new computer links are added or deleted. Hence, it allows for much more flexible expansion or contraction than many other proprietary network technologies. Its basic architecture encourages universal access and participation.

The Internet, then, should really be conceptualized as a flexible infrastructure. It is designed to maximize interoperability, that is, to be completely independent of software programs, hardware platforms, and other technologies. As a result, it is well suited to new applications and can easily accommodate revolutionary developments in both software and hardware. Because of its plasticity, however, it is naïve to assume that the Internet of today will be the Internet of the future. The architectures of cyberspace could conceivably undergo a major transformation in the next few years. As discussed in Chapter One, if the government chose to influence those architectures by mandating digital identity or otherwise controlling access through the Internet Service Providers (ISPs), cyberspace could become a very different place.

## ▶ The World Wide Web

The most recent surge in the Internet's popularity can be attributed to the emergence of the World Wide Web. The Web is essentially a service that runs over the Internet. The Web was developed at the European Particle Physics Lab as a means of exchanging data about high-energy physics among physicists scattered throughout the world. This group developed a standard known as *HTML,* or *Hypertext Markup Language,* which supports a procedure whereby "tags," or triggers, are attached to a word or phrase that links it to another document located anywhere on the Internet. The documents created by HTML can be in a multimedia format because they can include video, text, images, and even sound. Documents belong to a Web site that has a specific address, such as "www.bc.edu." The last three letters represent a "top level" identification (for example, *edu* stands for education, and com stands for a commercial enterprise); the middle part of the name designates the actual site (*bc* = Boston College).

Net browsers, such as Navigator provided by Netscape (based on the original Mosaic model) or Microsoft's Internet Explorer, enable users to "explore" the Web rather effortlessly. They are highly versatile navigational tools that enable users to access, display, and print documents; they also give users the ability to link to other documents at any location on the Web. Hyperlinks can create a maze of interconnected documents and Web sites that can sometimes confuse users but that can also greatly expand opportunities for research and investigation.

Despite its brief history, the World Wide Web itself has already become a vast, tangled network. Web sites now proliferate throughout cyberspace at schools and universities, hospitals, corporations, and many other organizations. Even individuals or small businesses have established their own Web pages. These Web pages will undoubtedly be the vehicle for the acceleration of e-commerce and many other network-based activities like education or fund raising. Web-based marketing is beginning to show significant results, and as a consequence, ad banners and commercial messages can now be found in almost every region of cyberspace.

The plethora of Web sites has created a density of information that can make it difficult for users to locate a particular site. Search engines such as those provided by Yahoo can help in this process, but even they are often ineffectual in the face of such voluminous data. Part of the problem, of course, is that the Web is just too large and too volatile to index properly. The Web already contains more than 320 million pages, but only a small fraction of these pages can be located by search engines.

In addition to search engines, users are increasingly relying on the assistance of portals, which are gateways or starting points on the Web. These portals assist users in orienting themselves amid the welter of Web sites available. Portals provide an array of services that include search engines, chat rooms, news, and so forth. Some predict that they will eventually control the ordinary user's experience of the Web.

Regardless of the difficulties that users encounter trying to navigate their way through cyberspace, the Web continues to rapidly gain in popularity. It is quickly becoming its own unique institution, taking the place of libraries, print catalogs, and even traditional news media for many users. It can be a rich source of research, news and information, and entertainment. And as more and more users develop their own sites, it has helped bring about the democratization of information predicted by many Internet visionaries.

## ▶ Electronic Commerce

*E-commerce* is a broad term that encompasses any form of business-related computer-to-computer transactions accomplished by means of telecommunications networks. It includes "processing of a growing variety of transactions, ranging from electronic data interchange—the well-established handling of business-to-business purchase orders, invoicing and other routine documents—to electronic payment systems, credit cards, and, most recently, sales of goods and services."[7] The term is now used almost exclusively to describe Internet commerce. The economics of the Internet clearly favor the migration of many forms of business from the physical realm to the realm of cyberspace.

Internet commerce in 1998 generated about $32 billion in revenues according to several research firms. The bulk of this was for business-to-business commerce, but $7.2 billion represented direct sales to consumers. Projections for e-commerce vary widely, but some estimate that on-line businesses could reach $1 trillion within the next ten years.[8]

According to Lynda Applegate, there are three basic forms of e-commerce: (1) customer-to-business, (2) business-to-business, and (3) interorganizational.[9] The last category normally involves the use of an intranet to disseminate information throughout the organization. Business-to-business applications are growing more common. For instance, e-commerce applications can greatly simplify cumbersome sourcing processes. Proctor&Gamble (P&G) is a major supplier of consumer goods to Wal*Mart, and the two companies recently implemented an automated, networked procurement system that sends inventory data to P&G, which then automatically ships goods to the appropriate Wal*Mart warehouse.

The fastest growth segment of e-commerce applications is customer-to-business, that is, downstream in the value chain in the areas of sales and marketing. More and more businesses are seeking to exploit the popularity of the Web by using it as a platform to communicate with their customers. The Internet is becoming a valuable tool for customer service because it can greatly accelerate the feedback mechanisms within most organizations. This can make companies much more resilient and more responsive to customer complaints or problems. It also provides corporations with important and timely feedback, which can help in many upstream activities such as product development.

The most explosive e-commerce application is direct sales to consumers. With 100 million people already on-line, the potential here is vast. For the consumer, the big attraction is convenience—with a single click of the mouse, an order for clothes, books, fine wine, or groceries can be placed at a Web site. For the retailer, a key advantage is lower costs: there may be a high initial investment for a computer system, but unlike traditional retailers, there is no need to continually invest in new stores and other physical assets to increase revenues.

E-commerce may not revolutionize the way goods are bought and sold, but by selling their wares on-line, vendors are creating a fairer market that simulates the model of perfect competition. This can be attributed to two phenomena: (1) greater access to information and (2) reduced barriers to entry. The wealth of information on-line about many products and services is helping overcome the information asymmetries that have been a typical and persistent market imperfection. Customers will be better able to use this data for comparison shopping. Furthermore, thanks to the diminished need for capital investment, there are lower barriers to entry in many markets that should pave the way for more competition. Both of these developments imply a slight shift in power to the consumer, which should ultimately translate into better service and lower prices.

Despite the success of companies like Amazon.com or eBay, the on-line auction company, many consumers are still reluctant to embrace e-commerce. Some fear becoming the victims of fraud or scams that are easier to execute because of the anonymous nature of Internet transactions. Others are concerned about the tenuous security of the Internet and worry that the price of convenience may be a loss of privacy. Unless consumers feel safe when they transact business on-line, e-commerce may never reach its full potential.

One major advantage of on-line commerce is the ability to customize sales and advertising to each individual consumer. A Web shopper's every move in cyberspace can be traced, allowing vendors to compile a profile of a consumer's preferences. According to *The Economist*, "With this feedback, online merchants can further differentiate themselves from their physical world competitors by customizing their shop or service for each customer."[10]

The on-line book dealer, Amazon.com, uses collaborative-filtering technology, which enables it to analyze a customer's purchases and to suggest other books the customer might like based on what people with similar purchase histories have bought. At the same time, Amazon.com offers a much broader selection of books than retail book chains. Eventually this powerful combination of customized service and broad product selection will attract many more customers and help fuel the growth of on-line commerce. Of course, knowledge of the customer's purchase history could lead to an infringement of privacy rights if it is sold to third parties without the customer's permission. We discuss those possibilities and their ethical ramifications in more depth in Chapter Five.

Although e-commerce Web sites have made the greatest progress in the United States, they are also proliferating in many other countries such as China. The Chinese government has encouraged the private sectors to develop Web-based businesses, and entrepreneurs are responding enthusiastically. As these sites gain in popularity, they could transform China's outdated retail business and enable manufacturers to automate purchases from suppliers. According to *Business Week,* "the global implications of this are enormous—as Web-based e-commerce spreads, traders around the world could link directly with suppliers and retailers across China."[11] Chinese language portals such as Sina.com and China.com are also emerging to serve as gateways to the Internet for Chinese citizens.

The Internet can never return to its halcyon days when it was frequented only by technology buffs and by academic researchers who formed an intimate and knowledgeable on-line community. As e-commerce intensifies, the Internet will continue to evolve, and to a large extent its future is in the hands of many different stakeholders who were not involved in the Internet's early days and who have a much more pragmatic and profit-oriented attitude about the Internet than its early founders.

## ▶ The Internet's Stakeholders

Stakeholder analysis has emerged as a powerful tool for dealing with many issues in strategic management and social responsibility. It can help companies appreciate their "nonmarket" responsibilities to various constituencies. A *stakeholder* is defined as any group or individual who can affect or is affected by the achievement of the corporation's objectives. What does it mean precisely to have a "stake" in something? According to Edward Freeman, there are three types of stakes. The first involves having an equity or ownership stake; obviously, corporate shareholders have this sort of equity stake. The second is an economic, or "market," stake that stems from the fact that the organization's actions can have a direct economic impact on the stakeholder. Employees would fall in this category. The third type of stake entails "being an influencer," or a "kibbitzer."[12] According to Dill, an influencer is "someone who has an interest in what the firm does because it affects [him or her] in some way, even if not directly in marketplace terms."[13] The Internet does not really have any owners, so the first sort of stake is irrelevant. However, many groups have substantial economic or kibbitzer stakes in the Internet's future.

As we have indicated, the Internet lacks a center: there is no central global authority or governing body that is the ultimate source of its rules or policies. And, of course, the Internet is a technological infrastructure, not an organization. Thus, it is not intelligible to speak of the Internet's obligations to stakeholders in the same way that we would speak of General Motors obligations to its stakeholders. Nonetheless, many constituencies now have an enormous stake or economic interest in this infrastructure. These constituencies depend heavily on the continued vitality and viability of the Internet. Other groups are marginally affected by the Internet's encroachment on basic activities, such as recreation or education.

The status of the Internet as a decentralized infrastructure implies that we engage in stakeholder analysis primarily from the focal point of the stakeholders themselves—what are their interests and concerns about the Internet, and what obligations are engendered by their particular use of the Internet? Furthermore, we contend that those who are active on the Internet and who have the capacity to influence this infrastructure in some way must take the interests of these other stakeholder groups into account if they want to behave in a socially responsible manner.

As the Internet's influence continues to expand, almost everyone will have some sort of stake in the Internet. We will consider here some representative groups, including individual users and households, the media, governments, corporations, nonprofit and research organizations, interest groups devoted to Internet issues, and finally the ISPs and other software companies that make it possible to surf the 'net or engage in electronic commerce (Figure 1). This is not necessarily an exhaustive list, but it does represent the Internet's major constituencies at this point.

The first group of stakeholders is composed of individual users and households who use the Internet increasingly for entertainment, e-mail, on-line shopping, and education. This group is becoming increasingly dependent on the Internet, and their concerns range from privacy and security issues to the ready availability of pornographic Web sites that might be easily accessible to children in these households. Consumers enjoy the convenience of on-line shopping, but they want to be assured that their transactions are secure and that their privacy rights are not compromised.

The second group consists of ISPs such as America Online (AOL) and Qwest, which make the Internet available to corporate and individual users. We include in this category other software companies such as Netscape, which make software for the Web such as browsers or applications software that make it possible to set up a Web site for on-line sales and marketing. Given the economic opportunities we have been discussing, a large segment of the software industry has a substantial economic interest in the Internet. Also included are those companies that provide the Internet's infrastructure, such as telecommunications firms like AT&T and MCI. These firms will play a key role in maintaining a state of the art telecommunications system that will better serve the needs of the Internet economy.

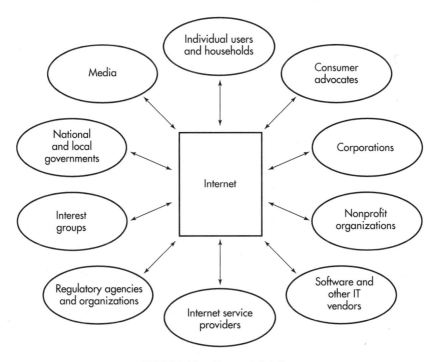

**FIGURE 1** Selected Internet Stakeholders

In the third group, we include corporations that now use the Internet for multifarious purposes. In some companies, the Internet serves as the backbone of a corporate intranet. It is also used extensively for e-mail applications and Web-based e-commerce. In addition, the automation and networking of relationships between corporations and their customers and suppliers is changing the way goods and services are bought and sold. It is now routine for companies to transmit orders and receive invoices electronically. Thus, corporations have a major economic stake in this global network because they are relying on it to help streamline supply chain activities, speed inventory turnover, and reduce cycle times. All of this helps contain costs and enhance revenue growth.

The fourth stakeholder group consists of all other nonprofit organizations, including libraries, schools and universities, hospitals, and private research organizations. Although they do not use the Internet for profit-based purposes, many of them also have a strong economic stake in the 'net, which is heavily relied on for fund rasing and recruitment purposes. Universities, for example, now use Web sites to attract students and to accept on-line applications, which are much less expensive to process.

The fifth group is the media. The traditional media brands such as *The New York Times* and *NBC* currently dominate news reporting on the

Internet. These organizations have built sophisticated Web sites that report news events 24 hours a day. The Internet has also spawned new media players such as the Drudge Report and other on-line news services that report and comment on the news from a particular political perspective. The Internet clearly creates a dynamic, new model for the dissemination of newsworthy information. This became especially evident to people when the Starr report was distributed on-line and was perused by millions of users within minutes after its official release from Congress.

Many questions have been raised about the reliability of Web journalism because the tendency has been to report stories on the Web before full verification. It is also more difficult to correct inaccurate information on the Web because stories can be downloaded and quickly sent out all over the 'net, making retraction almost impossible. Despite these issues, the media will certainly help shape the Internet's image as a reliable information source. At the same time, the media realizes that it has an enormous stake in this new revolutionary tool for propagating the news.

The sixth major Internet constituency consists of diverse interest groups that have a classic "kibbitzer" stake in the Internet. Their charge is to influence policies and regulations pertaining to the Internet, but they usually do not have a direct economic stake in the Internet. Included in this category are the following organizations: Computer Professionals for Social Responsibility, the Center for Democracy and Technology, Electronic Privacy Information Center (EPIC), and the Center for Media Education. There are also industry trade groups that do have an economic stake in the Internet. These groups lobby for Internet policies that will help their respective industries. The Direct Marketing Association (DMA) and the Interactive Services Association are trade groups that fight against government regulation of business-related Internet activities. The DMA, for example, is opposed to regulation of unsolicited e-mail, although it recognizes that such mail must be "cleaned up and legitimized."[14]

The seventh and final group is the "state," that is, the national and local governments of the many countries all over the world that have Internet access. For the United States, this includes the government agencies such as the FTC and FCC, which have some regulatory authority over the Internet, although the scope of that authority is far from clear. Every sovereign power is affected in some way by the Internet. Even the government of Saudi Arabia clearly recognizes the need to give its citizens access to and to be part of the Internet economy, but it resists unfettered Internet access, which might undermine its insular religious culture. As a result, the Saudi government has developed an archetypal filtering system that will ideally prevent all users in their country from gaining access to prohibited Web sites, such as ones that display pornographic material.

This stakeholder model, which will be referred to often in future chapters, is especially useful for several reasons. It compels those who will be making critical decisions about the Internet to coordinate their strategic plans with the legitimate needs and rights of the Internet's primary constituencies. Indeed, it can be plausibly argued that there is a moral obligation to deploy Internet-related technologies and to develop rules and policies for cyberspace in a conscientious manner that manifests respect for the rights and legitimate interests of these stakeholders. This includes developing architectures for the Internet that can also control behavior and shape the social environment of cyberspace.

As we observed earlier, the Internet is without a central organization that can make those decisions or set policies. Rather, at present, we have a community, or network, of stakeholders, and all of these groups have a *shared responsibility* to cooperate, when necessary, to respect the interests of each other and to safeguard the Internet's long-term viability.

## ▶ Internet Governance

The Web and the Internet have created many opportunities for data sharing and e-commerce, but they have also posed some formidable problems for lawmakers of national governments. The Internet has traditionally been decentralized and self-governing, and it has so far evaded strict or systemic regulations. However, although the Internet has always been an anarchic technology, there will always be a need for some type of stability imposed from above, that is, from the government or other centralized authorities. At a minimum, there must be a central body to manage Internet domain name distribution and to handle trademark disputes. But what exactly is the right mix of top-down regulations and bottoms-up control? To address this question, we should first consider the basic possibilities for Internet regulation.

There are at least three basic top-down models that have some plausibility and are worth a cursory review:

1. *Direct state intervention:* The existing laws of each nation can govern the Internet; thus, the state can amend or extend its current laws so that they apply to pertinent activities in cyberspace (the United States' recent Communications Decency Act legislation is an example of this approach).
2. *Coordinated international intervention:* A new intergovernmental organization composed of representatives from countries that use the Internet can establish new rules and regulations for cyberspace that will have international jurisdiction.
3. *Self-governance:* The 'net will develop its own semiofficial political structure; it will be governed by charters established by nonprofit organizations that represent the Internet's stakeholders.

Let's briefly enumerate some of the costs and benefits associated with adopting each of these three models. The premise underlying the first model is that the Internet is not a distinctive place that needs its own set of laws. The Internet is just another communications media, so a state's traditional legal structure may need some modification but is still applicable. Although this model has the benefit of simplicity because it does not require collaboration with other governments, enforcement would be a major problem. National borders simply do not have the same force and meaning when it comes to digitized information. In a complex digital world, it is often too difficult and time-consuming to track down and punish violators. Also, the state's laws can usually be easily evaded. For example, we mentioned Saudi Arabia's efforts to filter out objectionable international Web sites that violate its laws against pornography, which certainly extend to cyberspace. However, an astute user can call a server outside the country and print material via a country in Europe. In addition, regulation can often backfire by leading to "regulatory arbitrage." This occurs when companies or on-line vendors who are faced with stringent regulatory barriers at home shop around to find a more hospitable environment off shore.

The second model conceives of cyberspace as a unique and separate place with its own rules, established and enforced by a cooperative international organization not connected to a territorial government such as the United States. It would most likely have responsibility for mundane tasks such as domain name assignments, but it would also have the power to enforce international regulations such as restrictions on forbidden forms of speech. An international organization of this nature, analogous in some respects to the United Nations, with jurisdiction over the Internet, would certainly overcome some of the obstacles of the first model. Its authority would transcend geographical boundaries, and this would tend to curtail regulatory arbitrage and other evasive techniques.

However, this model also has some flaws. Johnson and Post raise a critical question about this mode of governance: "how could such a nongovernmental organization impose its rules on the Net as a whole?"[15] Also, by what authority could this organization successfully govern the 'net? Furthermore, there is no guarantee that this organization would not be captured by factions pushing an agenda based on their own vested interests. Thus, although this is an attractive alternative, the implementation problems and the attendant bureaucracy might render it a feckless and ineffectual solution in the long run.

Finally, according to the third model, the Internet would be self-governed by its own political and social structure suited for the unique problems posed in cyberspace. One possibility is to have activities on the Internet loosely controlled or coordinated by nonprofit international groups with specific charters. One charter might be developed to estab-

lish some common ground rules about e-commerce, and another charter might set some guidelines for intellectual property issues and trademark disputes.

The U.S. federal government seems to be leaning in this direction. It recently handed over control of the Internet Protocol number and domain
system to a private nonprofit organization called ICANN (Internet Corporation for Assigned Names and Numbers), whose charter is to look out
for the interests of the "Internet community." ICANN is a neutral governing body with limited powers that seeks to govern by gauging the consensus of Internet stakeholders on issues involving domain name
registrations. Many regard this effort to manage Internet addresses as a
critical test case for the efficacy of self-governance.

This third solution is not unworkable, but it too has some risks. The
primary problem is the lack of accountability. No one will have the
needed authority to force recalcitrant individuals or organizations to get
in line. Also, this system may be overrun by politics, with decisions being
made by insiders looking out for only their own selfish interests. If so, it
will be difficult to ensure that all of the relevant stakeholders have a real
voice in key decisions and controversial governance issues.

## ▶ Jurisdictional and Control Problems

Can the 'net *really* be controlled and regulated by the state? Many users
boast that the Internet by its very nature is virtually untamable and really
immune from such centralized controls, especially those that attempt to
suppress the flow of information. As Howard Rheingold writes, "Information can take so many alternative routes when one of the nodes of the
network is removed that the Net is almost immortally flexible. . . . The Net
interprets censorship as damage and routes around it."[16]

As we have seen, a fundamental problem with a particular sovereignty
imposing its will on the Internet is that laws and regulations are based on
geography; they have force only within a certain territorial area (for example, a state, a county, or a nation). As one jurist said: "All law is prima
facie territorial."[17]

Thus, because the Internet is a borderless global technology, it is almost
impossible for any country to enforce the laws or restrictions it seeks to
impose on this sprawling region of cyberspace. If the United States decides to outlaw pornography, it can enforce this restriction only among
U.S. purveyors of pornography. It cannot restrict vendors located in Europe or the Caribbean from making pornography available on the Internet for everyone to see. It can, of course, put the burden on Internet
providers and hold them liable for transmitting the illicit material no
matter where its source is located. But this seems to be an unfair and

unworkable solution because it is extremely difficult for ISPs to detect and properly filter all communications with pornographic elements. On the other hand, some court rulings in several countries have held ISPs liable for libelous material posted on their bulletin boards by subscribers, and this could be a precedent for holding ISPs liable for other problematic forms of speech.

Nonetheless, some governments have tried to regulate certain activities or forms of expression on the Internet, such as pornography, gambling, and hate speech. They have achieved mixed results. Singapore has been particularly repressive in its approach to regulating the Internet by imposing severe penalties on Internet providers for transmitting pornographic or seditious material. The Singaporean government has periodically searched the files of these providers and levied heavy fines when violations have been uncovered.

Despite its encouragement of Web-based business, the Chinese government is nervous about the Internet and has made it clear that "by linking with the Internet, we do not mean the absolute freedom of information."[18] Chinese officials use a fire wall to block access to pornographic and other objectionable Web sites such as those operated by human rights groups. China's iron grip on political discourse has been tested by Internet access, but China has responded with its usual heavy-handed and repressive tactics. It recently arrested and convicted a thirty-year-old computer executive for giving Chinese e-mail addresses to "hostile foreign publications." One such publication is VIP Reference, which sends e-mail reports on dissident activities within China. The executive argued, to no avail, that e-mail addresses are public information not subject to state control.

Thus, the ascendancy of this global computer network *appears* to be undermining the power of local governments to assert control over behavior within their borders. In addition, these futile efforts to regulate the Internet from a specific locality underscore the local sovereign's incapacity "to enforce rules applicable to global phenomena."[19] Perhaps those predictions that the Internet will cause an irreversible decline in national sovereignty are not so far-fetched.

Another problem emanates from the Net's empowerment of the individual through its code. Thanks to encryption programs, for example, it is more difficult for the state to conduct surveillance on confidential electronic communications. Similarly, filtering technologies give individuals the power to determine the content and format of the information they wish to receive. Electronic anonymity also frustrates lawmakers' efforts to hold individuals accountable for their on-line actions. The Internet is empowering the individual by the means of technology. It is shifting control from the state to the individual—a source of great consternation for many government leaders.

The individual's empowerment through code makes possible a more bottoms-up approach to regulation that many users and some civil libertarians favor. But can a case be made for letting the Internet organize and moderate itself as much as possible? According to David Post, "there are some problems on the Internet best solved by these messy, disordered, semi-chaotic, unplanned, decentralized systems, . . . and the costs that necessarily accompany such unplanned disorder may sometimes be worth bearing."[20] This messy bottoms-up approach described by Post is not a panacea for the Internet's various externalities, but it may be an adequate means of regulating conduct and addressing some of the social problems described in the following chapters.

There is surely much to be said for reliance on the constraints imposed by technology in the hands of individuals. In some ways, it seems preferable to the regulatory regime of government. It is nonintrusive, simpler, less expensive, and gives users the ultimate choice about what they want to see or do not want to see. Bottoms-up constraints also avoid the expensive government infrastructure that inevitably accompanies a regulatory scheme. In addition, this approach fits with the cultural shift now taking place in countries like the United States, whose citizens are increasingly antibureaucratic. Instead of reliance on bureaucracy and public policy to solve society's ills, many Americans now favor individual empowerment and local control.

As we observed in Chapter One, however, some legal scholars have perceptively made the case that sometimes technical solutions implemented by private parties can be more restrictive than actions taken by a democratic state. As Seth Finkelstein writes, "because of a perspective that might be rendered 'government action bad, private action good' there's great unwillingness to think about complicated social systems, or private parties acting as agents of censorship."[21]

In his critique of filtering systems such as PICS, Lawrence Lessig has made similar observations. PICS (Platform for Internet Content Selection) is a labeling standard that provides a way of labeling and blocking on-line material. It can be used by parents or schools to block access to a Web site with pornographic material or one filled with virulent hate speech. According to Lessig, the widespread deployment of this technology can yield a "tyranny of the code," as those in positions of authority impose their own standards on unsuspecting users.[22]

The power and potential of blocking software like PICS has not been lost on civil libertarians who have begun to better appreciate how these technologies can undermine the free flow of information far more effectively than government-imposed censorship. The threat to freedom may be more subtle and dispersed, but the result is still the sort of social domination, now effected by private parties, which the 'net is designed to resist.

The French philosopher Michel Foucault appreciated the import of this difference as well. In his writings on the nature of power, he differentiated between explicit state commands emanating from the sovereign power and a more covert and implicit exercise of domination. The latter normally has taken the form of surveillance, but it can take other forms as well. According to Foucault, "we have the emergence or rather the invention of a new mechanism of power possessed of a highly specific procedural technique. It is a type of power which is constantly exercised by means of surveillance rather than in a discontinuous manner by means of a system of levies or obligations distributed over time."[23] This clearly echoes Lessig's concern about the "tyranny of the code," a tyranny that can come from many different directions.

We are left then with a provocative but seminal question: should control and regulation of the Internet for the most part be left in the hands of private parties and the corrective technologies that they create and distribute in the marketplace? Or should we embrace a more top-down approach? Should the Internet be regulated more directly to contain its social costs without the collateral damage that can accompany the bottoms-up approach? Are the sinews of Internet stability best found in the rational laws and regulations emanating from a sovereign power or an international body?

## ▶ 'Net Governance and Ethics

At this stage of the Internet's rapid evolution, it would be presumptuous to predict which, if any, of these regulatory approaches might actually prevail. There will undoubtedly be some mixture of bottoms-up controls combined with top-down regulations. Some of those controls will likely come from self-governing bodies like ICANN, and others will come from state governments.

The real issue is how expansive a role the government should play in regulating the Internet. There is a case to be made that this role should be substantial given the importance of cyberspace for the future of commerce and for many other social activities. There is also wariness about the unpredictability of trusting the Internet to regulate itself. Without the government's sustained efforts to ensure a level playing field, companies like Microsoft and AOL could exert undue influence on e-commerce. Also, supporters of more extensive government regulations raise legitimate concerns about the poor state of efforts in the United States to regulate online privacy through self-control.

But can the government expand its regulatory role in the recalcitrant region of cyberspace? As we have seen, the state faces two formidable challenges in its efforts to regulate the Internet: (1) it must try to apply its own provincial laws to a global entity, and (2) it must contend with code that has radically empowered the individual. These obstacles appear to have weakened its sovereignty and given the individual the upper hand.

It would be naïve and premature, however, to underestimate the power of the state for controlling cyberspace. As Michel Foucault writes, "wherever there is power, there is resistance."[24] The state will certainly resist this state of affairs and seek to retrieve its lost dominance and diminished sovereignty. It may, for instance, use its vast power to tightly regulate ISPs or to demand that certain Internet architectures are structured in a certain way. Public policy makers also recognize the power of code as a constraint in cyberspace and might be willing to manipulate that code to counteract the difficulties of regulating cyberspace through fiat alone. As Lessig observes, the state will work to increase the very *regulability* of cyberspace by exercising control over its code.[25]

What we are left with, then, is a power struggle between a frustrated state and a newly empowered Internet community. At the epicenter of that struggle is the code of cyberspace. In many respects, the code is a far more effective constraint than law, norms, or the marketplace. One can envision many possibilities on both sides for using that code to gain control. For example, the architectures of the Internet currently facilitate electronic anonymity, but the state could respond by requiring that ISPs use code that mandates digital identity before one can even enter cyberspace.

What makes this struggle so perilous is the facility with which the code of the Internet can be manipulated. David Shapiro describes the Internet's capacity for empowering individual users as the "control revolution." He argues that the state's resistance to that revolution will "become more refined as governments become more adept at influencing code without running afoul of constitutional limitations or public opposition."[26]

The code is such a powerful regulator in the hands of the state or individuals because of its *malleability* and *obscurity*, its flexible ability to regulate or shape behavior gradually and inconspicuously. Code does not always constrain or influence behavior openly and directly in a way that is transparent to those it affects. This contrasts sharply with the constraint of law because the process of crafting laws through democratic procedures is subject to considerable public scrutiny.

Hence, the paramount importance of ethics in all of this. Although we do not take a stand on the preferability of a bottoms-up or a top-down regulatory philosophy, we contend that whatever approach becomes dominant, there must be careful attention paid to core human values such as autonomy, privacy, and liberty. Informal social controls abetted by technology may have the potential to provide effective and fair-minded regulations of cyberspace conduct, but only if those stakeholders involved are committed to *responsible* behavior. This will help minimize any negative effects on human rights that these corrective technologies (such as filtering) can bring about if they are improperly deployed.

Likewise, a top-down legislative process must be guided by these same core values. Governments must not overreact to the control revolution with restrictive laws or bypass the democratic process and manipulate Internet architectures to curtail basic human freedoms and rights merely for the sake of greater order and stability in cyberspace. They also must behave responsibly in their attempts to regulate cyberspace.

As we argued in Chapter One, what is of primary and utmost significance is the preservation in cyberspace of those transcendent human goods and moral values, which are so basic for the realization of human flourishing. *Moral values must be the ultimate regulator of cyberspace, not the code of engineers.* This will help ensure that abuses of the code will be kept to a minimum. If Internet stakeholders, including public policy makers, software developers, educators, and corporate executives, act prudently and responsibly, they will be vigilant and conscientious about respecting these values. As a result, they will find themselves guided by a moral wisdom that encourages care for others and a sense of measure concerning the public affairs of the Internet. This will also help achieve a reasonable equilibrium between the state and other Internet stakeholders.

In the next several chapters, we discuss what constitutes responsible approaches to cyberspace regulation. In the course of that discussion, we consider how code can be responsibly developed and used. We also focus on the right way for stakeholders to exercise their abundant power and on how these core moral values can be applied to some of the vexing dilemmas now emerging in cyberspace. The application of those values is not an exact science, though, and there will often be room for reasonable people to disagree. However, if there is a shared conviction that the Internet must be governed by these broad moral standards, it will be easier to resolve these inevitable conflicts. This is a complex topic that needs much more careful reflection along with an open and honest debate, which this book seeks to advance.

## Discussion Questions

1. In your own terms, explain the various regulatory models for controlling behavior on the Internet. Are there other possible models that have some validity?
2. Discuss the pros and cons of extensive government regulation of the Internet, either by a local sovereign government or by an international body specifically constituted for this purpose.
3. Evaluate the bottoms-up approach to regulation as it was presented in this chapter.
4. In what ways does the structure and present architecture of the Internet affect the choice of an optimal regulatory structure?

# References

1. Wren, C. 1997. Drug culture flourishes on Internet. *The New York Times,* June 20, p. A19.
2. Katz, J. 1997. Birth of digital nation. *Wired* April:186.
3. Rosenberg, G. 1997. Trying to resolve jurisdictional rules on the Internet. *The New York Times,* April 14, p. D1.
4. Agarwal, P. K. 1999. Building India's national Internet backbone. *Communications of the ACM* June:53–58.
5. The accidental superhighway: A survey of the Internet. *The Economist,* July 1, 1995, p. 6.
6. Zittrain, J. 1997. The rise and fall of sysopdom. *Harvard Journal of Law and Technology* 10:495.
7. Keen, P., et al. 1998. *The business Internet and intranets.* Cambridge, MA: Harvard Business School Press, p. 178.
8. Andes, G. 1998. The Internet—Why and where Internet commerce is succeeding. *The Wall Street Journal,* December 7, p. R4.
9. Applegate, L. 1995. *Electronic commerce: Trends and opportunities.* Cambridge, MA: Harvard Business School Publications.
10. Survey of electronic commerce. *The Economist,* May 10, 1997, p. 6.
11. Einhorn, B. 1999. China's Web masters. *Business Week* August 2, p. 49.
12. Freeman, R. E. 1984. *Strategic management: A stakeholder approach.* Marshfield, MA: Pittman, pp. 60–61.
13. Dill, W. 1975. Public participation in corporate planning: Strategic management in a kibbitzer's world. *Long Range Planning* 8(1):61.
14. See the Web site at www.the-dma.org.
15. Johnson, D., and Post, D. How shall the net be governed. Available at http://www.cli.org/X0025_LBFIN.html.
16. Rheingold, H. 1993. *The virtual community: Homesteading on the electronic frontier.* Reading, MA: Addison-Wesley, p. 7.
17. *America Banana Co. v. United Fruit Co.* 213 U.S. 347, 357 (1909).
18. Walker, T. 1995. China's wave of Internet surfers. *The Financial Times,* June 24.
19. Johnson, D., and Post, D. 1997. The rise of law on the global network. In Kahin, B., and Nesson, C. *Borders in cyberspace.* Cambridge: MIT Press, p. 6.
20. Post, D. G. 1999. *Of horses, black holes, and decentralized law-making in cyberspace.* Paper delivered at Private Censorship/Perfect Choice Conference at Yale Law School, April 9–11.
21. Finkelstein, S. 1998. Internet blocking programs and privatized censorship. *The Ethical Spectacle,* August, 1998 (http://www.spectacle.org/896/finkel.html).
22. Lessig, L. Tyranny in the infrastructure. p. 96.
23. Foucault, M. 1980. *Power and knowledge: selected interviews and other writings* Trans. C. Gordon. New York: Random House.
24. Foucault, M. 1978. *The history of sexuality,* vol. I. Trans. R. Hurley. New York: Vintage Books, p. 95.
25. Lessig, L. The laws of cyberspace. p. 11.
26. Shapiro, D. 1999. *The control revolution.* New York: Century Foundation Books, p. 73.

# CHAPTER THREE

# Free Speech and Content Control in Cyberspace

## ▶ Introduction

The Internet has clearly expanded the potential for individuals to exercise their First Amendment right to freedom of expression. The 'net gives all of its users a vast expressive power if they choose to take advantage of it. For example, users can operate their own bulletin boards, publish electronic newsletters, or establish a home page on the Web. According to Michael Godwin, the 'net "puts the full power of 'freedom of the press' into each individual's hands."[1] Or as the Supreme Court eloquently wrote in its *Reno v. ACLU* decision, the Internet enables an ordinary citizen to become "a pamphleteer, . . . a town crier with a voice that resonates farther than it could from any soapbox."[2]

As a result, the issue of free speech and content control in cyberspace has emerged as arguably the most contentious moral problem of the nascent Information Age. Human rights such as free speech have taken a place of special prominence in this century. In some respects, these basic rights now collide with the state's inclination to reign in this revolutionary power enjoyed by Internet users. Although the United States has sought to suppress on-line pornography, the target of some European countries, such as France and Germany, has been hate speech.

In addition, speech is at the root of most other major ethical and public policy problems in cyberspace, including privacy, intellectual property, and security. These three issues are discussed in future chapters where the free speech theme continues to have considerable saliency.

Restrictions on the free flow of information to protect privacy (such as the mandatory opt-in requirement in Europe) clearly amount to a restraint on the communication of information. Therefore, this effort to protect privacy is a notable free speech issue. Intellectual property rights are also tantamount to restrictions on free speech. If someone has property rights to a trademark, others cannot use that form of expression freely. Finally, one way in which users seek to secure their data is encryption, but encryption in the wrong hands could be a threat to national security, and therefore, many argue that encryption needs to be subject to government control. But shouldn't the right to free speech include the right to protect it from cybersnoopers by means of encryption? Thus, many of the most intractable difficulties in cyberspace can be reduced to the following question: what is the appropriate scope of free expression for organizations and individuals?

Those who pioneered Internet technology have consistently asserted that the right to free expression in cyberspace should have as broad a scope as possible. For many years, the government was reluctant to restrict or filter any form of information on the network for fear of stifling an atmosphere that thrives on the free and open exchange of ideas.

However, the increased use of the Internet, especially among more vulnerable segments of the population (such as young children), forced some public policy makers to rethink this laissez-faire approach. In the United States, the result has been several futile attempts to control Internet content through poorly crafted legislation. An unfortunate byproduct of this has been publicity and attention to this matter that is probably out of proportion to the depth or gravity of the problem.

Despite the calls for regulation, there is a powerful sentiment among many Internet stakeholders to maintain this status quo. The strongest voices continue to come from those who want to preserve the Internet's libertarian spirit and who insist that the surest way to endanger the vitality of this global network are onerous regulations and rules, which would stifle the creative impulses of its users and imperil this one last bastion of free, uninhibited expression.

In this chapter, we focus on those problematic forms of free expression, such as pornography, hate speech, and even the nuisance speech known as *spam* (unsolicited commercial e-mail). In the context of this discussion, we consider whether the libertarian ethic favoring broad free speech rights still has validity despite the growing complexity and the diverse user community now found in cyberspace.

## ▶ Pornography in Cyberspace

Before we discuss the U.S. Congress' recent efforts to regulate speech on the 'net we should be clear about what constitutes pornographic speech.

There are two broad classes of such speech: (1) obscene speech, which is completely unprotected by the First Amendment, and (2) "indecent" speech, which is not obscene for adults but should be kept out of the hands of children under the age of seventeen. In *Miller v. California* (1973), the Supreme Court established a three-part test to determine whether or not speech fell in the first category and was obscene for everyone. To meet this test, speech had to satisfy the following conditions: (1) it depicts sexual (or excretory) acts explicitly prohibited by state law; (2) it appeals to prurient interests as judged by a reasonable person using community standards; and (3) it has no serious literary, artistic, social, political, or scientific value. Child pornography is an unambiguous example of obscene speech.

The second class of speech, often called *indecent* speech, is obscene for children but not for adults. The relevant legal case is *Ginsberg v. New York,* which upheld New York's law banning the sale of speech "harmful to minors" to anyone under the age of seventeen. The law in dispute in the Ginsberg case defined *harmful to minors* as follows: "that quality of any description or representation, in whatever form, of nudity, sexual conduct, sexual excitement, or sado-masochistic abuse, when it: (1) predominantly appeals to the prurient, shameful, or morbid interests of minors, and (2) is patently offensive to prevailing standards in the adult community as a whole with respect to what is suitable for minors, and (3) is utterly without redeeming social importance for minors."[3] Although state legislatures have applied this case differently to their statutes prohibiting the sale of obscene material to minors, these criteria can serve as a general guide to what we classify as "Ginsberg" speech, which should be off limits to children under the age of seventeen.

## Public Policy Overview

### The Communications Decency Act (or CDA I)

The ubiquity of both forms of pornography on the Internet is a challenge for lawmakers. As the quantity of communications grows in the realm of cyberspace, there is a much greater likelihood that people will become exposed to forms of speech or images that are offensive and potentially harmful. If you are seeking to send an e-mail to the President of the United States and accidentally retrieve the Web site www.whitehouse.com instead of www.whitehouse.gov, you will see what we mean. By some estimates, the Internet currently has about 280,000 sites that cater to various forms of pornography, and some sources report that there is an average of an additional 500 sites coming on-line everyday, hence the understandable temptation of governments to regulate and control free expression on the Internet to contain the negative effects of unfettered free speech on this medium. The Communications Decency Act (CDA), recently ruled unconstitutional by the U.S. Supreme Court, represented one such futile, and some say misguided, attempt at such regulation.

One impetus behind the CDA was a flawed 1995 Carnegie Mellon study published in the Georgetown Law Review, which surveyed 917,410 computer images and found that 83.5% of all computerized photographs available on the Internet were pornographic. The Carnegie Mellon researchers also confirmed that on-line pornography was not only ubiquitous but also quite profitable for its many purveyors. In addition, those images were not just of naked women but involved pedophilia and paraphilia (images of bondage and sadomasochism). The results of this alarming study were reported in a famous *Time* magazine cover story titled "Cyberporn." According to the *Time* article, "The appearance of material like this on a public network accessible to men, women, and children around the world raises issues too important to ignore—or to oversimplify."[4]

The sensational *Time* article greatly heightened interest in the CDA. The bill's sponsor, Senator Exon, cited the Carnegie study as proof that passage of this legislation was essential. There was indisputable evidence, however, that parts of the study were spurious. Marty Rimm, a Carnegie Mellon undergraduate, was the study's lead researcher and author. The bulk of Rimm's data came from 68 bulletin board services (BBSs), some of which were adult BBSs, and yet Rimm certainly gave the impression that his study was based on and applied to the whole "information superhighway." According to Michael Godwin, "to generalize from commercial porn BBSs to the 'information superhighway' would be like generalizing from Times Square adult bookstores to the print medium."[5]

Nonetheless, thanks in part to the publicity generated by this study's findings and the *Time* cover story, The CDA, was passed by Congress and signed by President Clinton in 1996. Congress was especially worried about the direct negative effects of easily accessible pornographic material on children. It recognized that this medium erected few obstacles between gross and explicit material and curious children navigating their way through cyberspace. Congress also referred to a secondary effect: the ready availability of pornographic material might make parents less inclined to allow Internet use in their households, which would diminish the Internet's utility.

The CDA included several key provisions that restricted the distribution of sexually explicit material to children. It imposed criminal penalties on anyone who "initiates the transmission of any communication which is . . . indecent, knowing that the recipient of the communication is under 18 years of age." It also criminalized the display of patently offensive sexual material "in a manner available to a person under 18 years of age."[6]

Defenders of the CDA contended that this was an appropriate way of channeling pornographic or "Ginsberg" speech on the Internet away from children. It did not seek to ban adults from viewing such speech. Rather, it was an attempt to zone the Internet just as we zone physical environments. According to one supportive brief: "The CDA is simply a zoning ordinance for the Internet, drawn with sensitivity to the constitutional parameters the Court has refined for such regulation. The Act grants categorical defenses to those who reasonably safeguard indecent material from innocent children—who have no constitutional right to see it—channeling such material to zones of the Internet to which adults are welcome but to which minors do not have ready access."[7]

Support for the CDA was thin, however, and it was quickly overwhelmed by strident and concerted opposition. An alliance of Internet users, Internet Service Providers (ISPs), and civil libertarian groups challenged the legislation as a blatant violation of the First Amendment right of free speech. This coalition was spearheaded by the American Civil Liberties Union (ACLU) and the case became known as *ACLU v. Reno.*

The plaintiffs argued that because of the way the Internet worked, this law would most likely have the effect of also banning the transmission of "indecent" material to adults. They also contended that the banned speech might cast the net of censorship too far by including works of art and literature and maybe even health-related or sex education information.

Also, even if the CDA were enacted, it would have minimal impact on the availability of pornography in cyberspace. It could not control sexual content on the Internet originating in other countries, nor could it halt pornography placed on the Internet by anonymous remailers, which are usually located off shore and beyond the pale of U.S. regulators. The bottom line is that because the Internet is a global network, localized content restrictions enacted by a single national government to protect children from indecent material will probably be ineffectual.

A panel of federal judges in Philadelphia ruled unanimously that the CDA was a violation of the First and Fifth Amendments. The Justice Department appealed the case, which now became known as *Reno v. ACLU,* but to no avail. The Supreme Court agreed with the lower court's ruling, and in June 1997, it declared that this federal law was unconstitutional. The Court was especially concerned about the vagueness of this content-based regulation of speech. According to the majority opinion written by Justice Stevens, "We are persuaded that the CDA lacks the precision that the First Amendment requires when a statute regulates the content of speech. In order to deny minors access to potentially harmful speech, the CDA effectively suppresses a large amount of speech that adults have a constitutional right to receive and to address to one another."[8] Stevens also held that the free expression on the Internet is entitled to the highest level of First Amendment protection. This is in contrast to the more limited protections for other more pervasive media such as radio and broadcast and cable television, where the Court has allowed many government-imposed restrictions. In making this important distinction, the Court assumes that computer users have to actively seek offensive material, whereas they are more likely to encounter it accidentally on television or radio if it were so available.

## CDA II

Most of those involved in the defeat of the CDA realized that the issue would not soon go away. Congress, still supported by public opinion, was sure to try again. In October 1998, they did try again, passing an omnibus budget package that included the Child Online Protection Act (COPA), a successor to the original CDA, which has become known as CDA II. The law was signed by President Clinton, and like its predecessor, it was immediately challenged by the ACLU. CDA II would make it illegal for the operators of commercial Web sites to make sexually explicit materials harmful to minors available to those younger than seventeen years of age. Commercial Web site operators would be required to collect an identification code, such as a credit card number, as proof of age before allowing viewers access to such material.

The ACLU and other opponents claimed that the law would lead to excessive self-censorship. CDA II would have a negative impact on the ability of these commercial Web sites to reach an adult audience. According to Max Hailperin, "There is no question that the COPA impairs commercial speakers' ability to cheaply, easily, and broadly communicate material to adults that is constitutionally protected as to the adults (non-obscene), though harmful to minors."[9] The law is more narrowly focused than CDA I because it attempts to define objectionable sexual content more carefully. Such content would lack "serious literary, artistic, political or scientific value" for those younger than seventeen years of age. However, the law's critics contend that it is still worded too broadly. Those critics also worry about what will happen if the law is arbitrarily or carelessly applied. For example, would some sites offering sexual education information violate the law?

In February 1999, a Philadelphia federal judge issued a preliminary injunction against CDA II, preventing it from going into effect. This judge accepted the argument that the law would lead to self-censorship and that "such a chilling effect could result in the censoring of constitutionally protected speech, which constitutes an irreparable harm to the plaintiffs."[10] An appeal is considered likely, meaning that the ultimate resolution will have to await the Supreme Court's decision.

At the heart of the debate about the CDA and content regulation is the basic question that was raised in Chapter Two about how the Internet should be controlled. Should government impose the kind of central controls embodied in this legislation? Or should the Internet be managed and controlled through a more bottoms-up, user-oriented approach, with users empowered to develop their own solutions tailored to their own needs and value systems? One advantage of the latter approach is that such controls are more consistent with the Internet's decentralized network architecture. For many users, decentralism in the area of content control seems preferable to formal state regulations. It respects civil liberties and leaves the opportunity for content control in the hands of those most capable of exercising it.

However, reliance on a decentralized solution is certainly not without opposition and controversy. If we empower users to control Internet content in some ways, we are still left with many questions. If we assert that the purpose of censoring the Internet is the preservation of the community's values, how do we define *community*? Also, how do we ascertain what the community's values really are? Finally, can we trust technology to help solve the problem or will it make matters even worse?

## Automating Content Controls

Nonetheless, thanks to the rulings against CDA I and II, the burden of content control is now shifting to parents and local organizations. This communal power has raised some concerns. To what extent should local communities and institutions (such as schools, prisons, libraries, and so on) assume direct responsibility for controlling content on the Internet? Libraries, for example, must consider whether it is appropriate to use filtering software to protect young patrons from pornography on the Internet. Is this a useful and prudent way to uphold local community or institutional standards? Or does this sort of censorship compromise a library's traditional commitment to the free flow of ideas?

There are two broad areas of concern about the use of content controls that need elaboration. The first area concerns the ethical probity of censorship itself, even when it is directed at the young. There is a growing tendency to recognize a broad spectrum of rights, even for children, and to criticize parents, educators, and politicians who are more interested in imposing their value systems on others than in protecting vulnerable children. Jonathan Katz and other advocates of children's rights oppose censorship, even within a private household, unless it is part of a mutually agreed-upon social contract between the parent and child. According to Katz, "Parents who thoughtlessly ban access to online culture or lyrics they don't like or understand, or who exaggerate and distort the dangers of violent and pornographic imagery, are acting out of arrogance, imposing brute authority."[11] Rather, Katz contends, young people have a right to the culture that they are creating and shaping. The ACLU seems to concur with this position and it too advocates against censorship as a violation of children's rights.

Lurking in the background of this debate is the question of whether children have a First Amendment right to access indecent materials. Legal scholars have not reached a consensus about this, but if children do have such a right, it would be much more difficult to justify filtering out indecent materials in libraries or educational institutions. One school of thought about this issue is that a child's free speech rights should be proportionate to his or her age. The older the child, the more problematic are restrictions on indecent material.

The second area of concern pertains to the suitability of the blocking methods and other automated controls used to accomplish this censorship. Two basic problems arise with the use of blocking software. The first problem is the unreliability and lack of precision that typifies most of these products; there are no perfect or foolproof devices for filtering out obscene material. Programs like the popular SurfWatch operate by comparing Web site addresses to a list of prohibited sites that are known to contain pornographic material. SurfWatch currently prohibits more than 30,000 Web sites. However, this filtering program is less effective with Usenet newsgroups (electronic bulletin boards or chat rooms). SurfWatch depends on the name of the newsgroup to decide whether it should be banned; thus, an earlier version missed a chat room that displays pornographic material but goes under the name alt.kids-talk.penpals.

Another problem is that these blocking programs can be used to enforce a code of political correctness unbeknownst to parents or librarians who choose to install them. Sites that discuss AIDS, homosexuality, and related topics are routinely blocked by certain filtering programs. Often, these programs are not explicit or forthright about their blocking criteria, which greatly compounds this problem.

More sophisticated filtering mechanisms are appearing in the marketplace, which can obviate some of the precision problems associated with blocking programs. Consider, for example, the rating system, known as PICS (Platform for Internet Content Selection), that is rapidly gaining in popularity. PICS is more efficient and less expensive than blocking software. It is a framework that permits labeling of Internet content. It provides a standard format and supports multiple labeling schemes or rating services. Internet content providers can embed a label within their own Web site, or third parties could rate that Web site independently. In either case, a common labeling vocabulary is available for use. End users surfing the Web can rely on the author's label or the label provided by a third party. In some cases, of course, authors will be disinclined to label their own Web sites. Neo-Nazi sites, for example, typically do not have labels embedded within them. On the other hand, the Simon Wiesanthal Center, a nonprofit organization that combats anti-Semitism, could rate those Web sites based on the presence of anti-Semitic content and hate speech.

Labels can be embedded in Web documents or otherwise attached to a Web site or they can be stored in separate server. In the latter case a user could instruct the software to check for the labels on that server before accessing a particular site. Software can be programmed to take action based on a label such as blocking inappropriate, offensive Web sites. If a household wanted to prevent access to hateful, anti-Semitic Web sites, it could instruct its Internet browser to check a central server where those sites and other sites would be labeled. Any properly labeled anti-Semitic site, such as www.aryannation.org rated by a third party like the Simon Wiesanthal Center would also include an action code blocking access to that site.

The use of this labeling infrastructure has already generated significant controversy. PICS certainly has its supporters who argue that this voluntary system is far superior to one imposed by the government. They assert that filtering software devolves responsibility to the level where it should be in a pluralistic society, that is, with parents, schools, and local communities.

In contrast, civil libertarians and many responsible professionals strenuously object to the use of rating systems like PICS, claiming that it can transform the Internet into a virtual censorship machine. They worry that because rating is so labor intensive that a few rating systems will dominate and will exclude considerable questionable or controversial material. Restrictions inscribed into computer code end up having the force of law without the checks and balances provided by the legal system. With programs like PICS, we will be handing over regulation of the Internet to private enterprises, which can develop tendentious labeling schemes and thereby use filtering technologies to further their own particular political or social agendas.

This is indeed a striking example of how code is becoming a substitute for law as a constraint on cyberspace behavior. Thanks to the nullification of the CDA, Internet stakeholders in increasing numbers will resort to software that may be far more effective than the law in suppressing pornographic material.

Although some of the criticism directed at PICS and automated content control is exaggerated, the difficulties identified here should not be underestimated. At the same time, a more imperceptible problem with filtering systems is that they can be used to tailor and personalize one's perception of reality—to control one's environment in a detrimental way that narrows one's perspectives and experience. According to Cass Sunstein, "Each person could design his [or her] own communications universe. Each person could see those things that he [or she] wanted to see, and only those things."[12]

Finally, a potential disadvantage of PICS is that the filter can be imposed at any level in the vertical hierarchy that controls the accessibility of Internet services. It can be invoked at the individual user level, the corporate or institutional level, the ISP level, or even the state level. It can be used by the Chinese to limit public discourse about democracy just as easily as it can be used by parents to keep pornographic Web sites far from the curious gaze of their children. There is significant opportunity for abuse, making many conscientious stakeholders apprehensive about its adoption.

Although we take no position on the merits of PICS, we do contend that users who embrace this method of dealing with cyberporn should deploy this software responsibly to minimize any potential for collateral damage. If this code is designed, developed, and used *prudently*, we may find that it has the wherewithal to create the desired effect with minimal negative impact on individual liberties or the common good.

So, what constitutes responsible use of these automated access codes? Let's suggest a few criteria. First, the use of PICS or other automated content controls should be strictly voluntary—parents or schools should be allowed to choose whether to restrict Web content, while authors can choose whether to label their Web sites. In contrast, a mandatory rating and filtering system administered or sponsored by the government would be problematic and imprudent. It would impose a uniform solution to what has always been regarded as a local problem. Second, a Web site that does choose to use a label must have the integrity to label itself accurately. Third, third parties that rate Web sites must strive to provide fair, accurate, and consistent ratings that are subject to reasonable external scrutiny. They must be flexible enough to judiciously handle appeals from Web sites that maintain that they have been mislabeled. Fourth, there should be an adequate transparency level in blocking software of rating schemes. Although some information may be proprietary, labeling services must be as up front as possible about their labeling philosophy and their general standards of exclusion. CyberSitter, for example, which purports to protect children from pornography, blocks the Web site of the National Organization for Women. Such blocking is irresponsible unless this rating service also has a political agenda that it explicitly reveals to its patrons. Finally, PICS should not be adopted as a high-level centralized filtering solution. Filtering should occur only at the lowest levels of the hierarchy. It should not be used by search engines, ISPs, or states to censor the Internet; this is especially harmful if it is done in a surreptitious and dogmatic fashion.

Even if automated content controls such as PICS are used responsibly and diligently, their use still raises some troubling questions. Will there be chaos on the Internet as many different private and public groups express opinions about Web sites in the form of content labels? Should there be any restrictions on the provision of such labels? But aren't restrictions on content labels tantamount to restrictions on free speech? And which local institutions should assume the burden of implementing filtering technologies?

We cannot consider all of these question here, but the complex issues involved in the last question clearly emerge in the controversial debate about the use of filtering devices in libraries. Both public and private libraries face a real dilemma: they can either allow unfettered Internet access even to their youngest patrons or use filtering products to protect minors from pornographic material.

Libraries that favor the first approach argue that the use of filtering devices compromises the library's traditional commitment to the free flow of information and ideas. Some of this opposition to these filtering devices originates from the imprecise way in which they function. The public library in New York City subscribes to this philosophy and presently does not use filtering devices. Furthermore, the American Library Association (ALA) is opposed to the installation of filters and endorses the idea of unrestricted Internet access for both adults and minors.

Some librarians, however, disagree with the ALA. They maintain that the Internet should be censored and that filtering programs provide a way to support and reinforce local community values. According to Brenda Branch, the director of the Austin Public Library in Texas, "We have a responsibility to uphold the community standard. . . . We do not put pornographic material in our book collection or video collection, and I also don't feel we should allow pornographic materials in over the Internet."[13]

In Loudon County, Virginia, the public library decided (after some soul searching) to install X-Stop, which blocks access to a list of predetermined pornographic Web sites. In response, the ACLU sued the library on behalf of eight plaintiffs whose Web sites were blocked by X-Stop. According to the ACLU, blocking these sites violates the right to free speech and is akin to banning books. This suit has been regarded by many as a key test of the legitimacy of constraining one's freedom to use the Internet.

Everyone recognizes the novelty of cases such as Loudon County, as the legal system struggles to find the most appropriate analogy. Opponents of filtering, for example, argue that blocking Internet sites is analogous to the library's purchase of an encyclopedia and the deletion of certain articles that do not meet its decency standard. The other side contends that access to a Web site is more akin to a request for an interlibrary loan, which the library is not required to satisfy.

The case went through several stages, and in November 1998, a federal judge sided with the ACLU, ruling that the libraries' policy of using filtering software on all of its computers "offends the guarantee of free speech in the First Amendment." There is little doubt that this decision will be a critical precedent and will probably make most libraries less likely to rely on filters.

One compromise and common-sense position used by the Boston Public Library is the installation of filtering devices on children's computers but not on those in the adult areas. Still, the ALA and the ACLU do not favor this type of zoning approach. As the result of an ACLU lawsuit, the library system in Kern County, California, was forced to abandon such a zoning plan and to give all of its patrons, including minors, the right to use a computer without a filter. Moreover, this solution contradicts Article 5 of the ALA's Library Bill of Rights: "A person's right to use a library should not be denied or abridged because of origin, age, background, or views."[14] According to the ALA, this article precludes the use of filters on *any* computer systems within a library.

How should these nettling matters be resolved? Let's assume for the sake of argument that filtering devices and systems (like PICS) do become more precise and accurate. If filtering is more dependable and blocking criteria more transparent, should libraries and other institutions give priority to the value of free expression and the free flow of ideas and information, no matter how distasteful some of that information is or do they give priority to other community values at the expense of the unimpeded flow of information?

By following the first option and not regulating the Internet at the local level, we are giving the First Amendment its due—letting all voices be heard, even those that are sometimes rancorous and obscene. One can base this decision on several principles: the rights of children to access indecent material, the notion that censorship should not replace the cultivation of trust, and the education of individuals to act guardedly in cyberspace. Moreover, the occasional abuse of the Internet in a school or library setting should not be a reason to censor the entire network. Censorship is a disproportionate response to isolated incidents of abuse.

The argument for reliance on education and trust to solve this problem is a compelling one. Shouldn't schools and libraries attempt to *educate* students and young patrons about Internet use and abuse? But as Richard Rosenberg argues, "if the first instinct is to withhold, to restrict, to prevent access, what is the message being promulgated?"[15] If institutions such as schools and libraries truly value the ideals of trust, openness, and freedom, imposing censorship on information is a bad idea that mocks those ideals. Also, wouldn't such restrictions start us down a dangerous slide to more pernicious forms of censorship and repression? How and where do we draw the line once we begin to restrict access to Internet content? As a result, many free speech proponents argue that this global medium of expression deserves the highest level of protection a pluralistic society and its institutions can possibly offer.

Many other compelling and persuasive arguments can be made for keeping the Internet a free and open medium of exchange. There is something satisfying about the Chinese government's impotence to completely control free expression in this medium as they now control other forms of political dissent. The Internet can thereby become a wonderful vehicle for spreading the ideals of democracy. It is surely not the ally of tyrants or the enemies of democracy.

But should *all* information be freely accessible to anyone who wants it? Is this a rational, morally acceptable, and prudent policy? What are the costs of living in a society that virtually absolutizes the right to free speech in cyberspace and makes all forms of speech readily available even to its youngest members?

Because these costs can be high, it is critically important to consider the other side of this issue. Many responsible moralists contend that some carefully formulated, *narrow* restrictions on specific types of indecent speech are perfectly appropriate when young children are involved.

They maintain that parents, schools, libraries, and other local institutions have an obligation to promote and safeguard their own values as well as the values of their respective communities. This is part of the more general obligation to help promote public morality and the public order. Freedom and free expression are critically important human rights, but these and other rights can be reasonably exercised only in a context of mutual respect and common acceptance of certain moral norms, which are often called the *public morality*. In any civilized society, some of these norms entail sexual behavior and especially the sexual behavior of and toward children. Given the power of sexuality in one's life, the need for carefully integrating sexuality into one's personality, and the unfortunate tendency to regard others as sexual objects of desire (rather than as human beings), there is a convincing reason for fostering a climate in which impressionable children can be raised and nurtured without being subjected to images of gross or violent sexual conduct that totally depersonalize sexuality, exalt deviant sexual behavior, and thereby distort the view of responsible sexual behavior. This is clearly an aspect of the common good and public morality and is recognized as such by public officials in diverse societies who have crafted many laws (such as the law against the production of child pornography) to protect minors and to limit the exercise of rights in this area. Hence, given the importance of protecting young children as best as we can from psychologically harmful pornographic images, parents and those institutions that function *in loco parentis* should not be timid about carefully controlling Internet content when necessary.[16]

It is never easy to advocate censorship at any level of society precisely because the right to free expression is so valuable and cherished. However, proponents of automated content controls argue that all human rights, including the right to free expression, are limited by each other and by other aspects of the common good, which can be called *public morality*. According to this perspective, parents and schools are acting prudently when they choose to *responsibly* implement filtering technologies to help preserve and promote the values of respect for others and appropriate sexual conduct that are part of our public morality. Preserving free speech and dealing with sexually explicit material will always be a problem in a free and pluralistic society, and this is one way of achieving a proper balance when the psychological health of young children is at stake.

## ▶ Other Forms of Problematic Speech

### Hate Speech

The rapid expansion of hate speech on the Web raises similar problems and controversies. Many groups, such as white supremacists and anarchists, have Web sites that advocate their particular point of view. Some of these sites are blatantly anti-Semitic, whereas others are dominated by Holocaust revisionists who claim that the Holocaust never happened. On occasion, these sites can be especially virulent and outrageous, such as the Web site of the Charlemagne Hammerskins. The first scene reveals a man disguised in a ski mask who is bearing a gun and standing next to a swastika. The site has this ominous warning for its visitors: "Be assured, we still have one-way tickets to Auschwitz."

Some hate Web sites take the form of computer games, such as Doom and Castle Wolfenstein, which have been constructed to include African-Americans, Jews, or homosexuals as targets of violence. In one animated game, the Dancing Baby, which became a popular television phenomenon, has been depicted as the "white power baby."

In the United States, the most widely publicized of these hate speech sites are those that attack doctors who perform abortions. Some of these sites are especially menacing and venomous, such as "The Nuremberg Files," which features a "Wanted" list of abortion doctors. The site's authors contend that they are not advocating violence but only expressing their opinion, albeit in a graphic format.

What can be done about this growing subculture of hate on the Internet? The great danger is that the message of hate and bigotry, once confined to reclusive, powerless groups, can now be spread more efficiently in cyberspace. Unlike obscenity and libel, hate speech is not illegal under U.S. federal law and is fully protected by the First Amendment. Even speech that incites hatred of a particular group is legally acceptable. The only exception to this is the use of "fighting words," which were declared beyond the purview of the First Amendment by the Supreme Court. Such speech, however, must threaten a clear and present danger. In the controversial case of the antiabortion Web sites, a federal court recently ruled that the site's content was too intimidating and hence was not protected by the First Amendment. But in general, censorship of on-line hate speech is inconsistent with the First Amendment.

On the other hand, in European countries like Germany and France, anti-Semitic, Nazi-oriented Web sites are illegal. In Germany, the government has required ISPs to eliminate these sites under the threat of prosecution. Critics of this approach argue that it is beyond the capability of ISPs to control content in such a vast region as the World Wide Web. It is also illegal for Internet companies to ship Nazi materials into Germany. This means that Amazon.com should not be selling books like Hitler's *Mein Kampf* to its German customers, although this restriction too will be difficult to enforce.

Although government regulation and explicit laws about hate speech are suitable for some countries, an alternative to government regulation is once again reliance on user empowerment and *responsible* filtering that does not erroneously exclude legitimate political speech. Parents and certain private and religious institutions might want to seize the initiative to shield young children and sensitive individuals from some of this material such as virulent anti-Semitism.

However, even more caution must be exercised in this case because the distinction between hate speech and unpopular or unorthodox political opinion is sometimes difficult to make. A rule of thumb is that hate speech Web sites are those that attack, insult, and demean whole segments of the population, such as Jews, Italians, African-Americans, whites, homosexuals, and so forth. Many sites will fall in a nebulous gray area, and this will call for conscientiousness and discretion on the part of those charged with labeling those sites.

## Anonymous Speech

Anonymous communication in cyberspace is enabled largely through the use of anonymous remailers, which strip off the identifying information on an e-mail message and substitute an anonymous code or a random number. By encrypting a message and then routing that message through a series of anonymous remailers, a user can rest assured that his or her message will remain anonymous and confidential. This process is called *chained remailing*. The process is effective because none of the remailers will have the key to read the encrypted message; neither the recipient nor any remailers (except the first) in the chain can identify the sender; the recipient cannot connect the sender to the message unless every single remailer in the chain cooperates. This would assume that each remailer kept a log of their incoming and outgoing mail, which is highly unlikely.

According to Michael Froomkin, this technique of chained remailing is about as close as we can come on the Internet to "untraceable anonymity," that is, "a communication for which the author is simply not identifiable at all."[17] If someone clandestinely leaves a bunch of political pamphlets in the town square with no identifying marks or signatures, that communication is also characterized by untraceable anonymity. In cyberspace, things are a bit more complicated, and even the method of chained remailing is not foolproof: if the anonymous remailers do join together in some sort of conspiracy to reveal someone's identity, there is not much anyone can do to safeguard anonymity.

Do we really need to ensure that digital anonymity is preserved, especially since it is so often a shield for subversive activities? It would be difficult to argue convincingly that anonymity is a core human good, utterly indispensable for human flourishing and happiness. One can surely conceive of people and societies where anonymity is not a factor for their happiness. However, although anonymity may not be a primary good, it is surely a secondary one because *for some people in some circumstances,* a measure of anonymity is important for the exercise of their rational life plan and for human flourishing. The proper exercise of freedom, and especially free expression, requires the support of anonymity in some situations. Unless the speaker or author can choose to remain anonymous, opportunities for free expression become limited for various reasons and that individual may be forced to remain mute on critical matters. Thus, without the benefit of anonymity, the value of freedom is constrained.

We can point to many specific examples in support of the argument that *anonymous free expression* deserves protection. Social intolerance may require some individuals to rely on anonymity to communicate openly about an embarrassing medical condition or an awkward disability. Whistleblowers may be understandably reluctant to come forward with valuable information unless they can remain anonymous. And political dissent even in a democratic society that prizes free speech may be impeded unless it can be done anonymously. Anonymity then has an incontestable value in the struggle against repression and even against more routine corporate and government abuses of power. In the conflict in Kosovo, for example, some individuals relied on anonymous programs (such as anonymizer.com) to describe atrocities perpetrated against ethnic Albanians. If the Serbians were able to trace the identity of these individuals, their lives would have been in grave danger.

Thus, although there is a cost to preserving anonymity, its central importance in human affairs is certainly beyond dispute. It is a positive good; that is, it possesses positive qualities that render it worthy to be valued. At a minimum, it is valued as an instrumental good, as a means of achieving the full actualization of free expression.

Anonymous communication, of course, whether facilitated by remailers or by other means, does have its drawbacks. It can be abused by criminals or terrorists seeking to communicate anonymously to plot their crimes. It also permits cowardly users to communicate without civility or to libel someone without accountability and with little likelihood of apprehension by law enforcement authorities. Anonymity can also be useful for revealing trade secrets or violating other intellectual property laws. In general, secrecy and anonymity are not beneficial for society if they are overused or used improperly. According to David Brin, "anonymity is the darkness behind which most miscreants—from mere troublemakers all the way to mass murderers and would-be tyrants—shelter in order to wreak harm, safe against discovery or redress by those they abuse."[18]

Although we admit that too much secrecy is problematic, the answer is not to eliminate all secrecy and make everything public and transparent, which could be the inevitable result of this loss of digital anonymity. Nonetheless, it cannot be denied that anonymity has its disadvantages and that digital anonymity and an unfettered Internet can be exploited for many forms of mischief. Therefore, governments are tempted to sanction the deployment of architectures that will make Internet users more accountable and less able to hide behind the shield of anonymity.

Despite the potential for abuse, however, there are cogent reasons for eschewing the adoption of those architectures and protecting the right to anonymous free speech. A strong case can be put forth that the costs of banning anonymous speech in cyberspace are simply too high in an open and democratic society. The loss of anonymity may very well diminish the power of that voice that now resonates so loudly in cyberspace. As a result, regulators must proceed with great caution in this area.

## Student Web Sites

At Westlake High School in Ohio, a student, Sean O'Brien, felt that he was being unfairly treated by one of his teachers. His response was to create a home Web page that included a photograph of his music teacher, who was described as "an overweight middle-age man who doesn't like to get haircuts." The High School was outraged and promptly took action. It suspended O'Brien for ten days, ordered him to delete the Web site, and threatened his expulsion if he failed to comply. His parents filed suit against the school district, claiming that this order infringed on their son's right to free speech.

The central question in the case revolves around the school's right to discipline a student for the contents of a personal Web site. According to the ACLU and other legal scholars, who supported O'Brien's lawsuit, a school's efforts to exercise control of home Web sites, what students say outside of school, no matter how outrageous it may be, seems inconsistent with the First Amendment right to free expression. According to this view, students have every right to use the Internet to criticize their schools or their teachers.

The legal precedent on the issue is somewhat ambiguous. The U.S. Supreme Court has recognized three types of control over student speech. First, schools can control the content of student newspapers or other student publications such as those associated with extracurricular activities. Second, they can control and seek to curtail profane speech that occurs within the school. Third, they can regulate off-campus speech if that speech causes a "material and substantial" disruption of the school's classroom activities. The third criteria is obviously the only one that may be apposite in this case. Does O'Brien's criticism of his teacher constitute a material disruption? A marginal case can be made perhaps that because the site was read by many of O'Brien's classmates, the music teacher's class was "disrupted." However, embarrassing remarks aimed at teachers are probably not what the Supreme Court had in mind. The disruptive activity would have to be much more serious to warrant censorship of what a student says outside of the classroom.

In the O'Brien case, an out-of-court settlement was reached in April 1998, in which the O'Brien family was awarded $30,000 in damages. He also received an apology from the school district, which promptly reinstated him at Westlake High in good standing. The problem of controversial home Web sites will only get worse and may be a moderate but necessary price to pay for the information egalitarianism afforded to all computer users by the Internet. Schools must find a way to discourage student Web sites that mock teachers or indulge in profane insults by means other than censorship. A good starting point is a continued emphasis on the value of decent and civil speech in the realm of cyberspace.

## Spam as Commercial Free Speech

*Spam* refers to unsolicited, promotional e-mail, usually sent in bulk to thousands or millions of Internet users. Quite simply, it is junk e-mail that is usually a significant annoyance to its recipients. The major difference between electronic junk mail and paper junk mail is that the per copy cost of sending the former is so much lower. There are paper, printing, and postage charges for each piece of regular junk mail, but the marginal cost of sending an additional piece of junk e-mail is negligible. For example, some direct marketers who specializes in spam charge their clients a fee as low as $400 to send out several million messages.

But spam is not cost free. The problem is that the lion's share of these costs are externalities, that is, they are costs borne involuntarily by others. As Robert Raisch has observed, spam is "postage-due marketing."[19] The biggest cost associated with spam is the consumption of computer resources. For example, when someone sends out spam the messages must sit on a disk somewhere, and this means that valuable disk space is being filled with unwanted mail. Also, many users must pay for each message received or for each disk block used. Others pay for the time they are connected to the Internet, time that can be wasted downloading and deleting spam. As the volume of spam grows and commercial use of the Internet expands, these costs will continue their steady increase. Furthermore, when spam is sent through ISPs they must bear the costs of delivery. This amounts to wasted network bandwidth and the use of system resources such as disk storage space along with the servers and transfer networks involved in the transmission process.

In addition to these technical costs, there are also administrative costs. Users who receive these unwanted messages are forced to waste time reading and deleting them. If a vendor sends out 6 million messages and it takes 6 seconds to delete each one, the total cost of this one mailing is 10,000 person hours of lost time.

Purveyors of spam contend that this is simply another form of commercial free speech that deserves the same level of First Amendment protection as traditional advertising. They point out, perhaps correctly, that a ban on spam would be not only impractical but also unconstitutional because it would violate their constitutional right to communicate. The right to commercial forms of speech has stood on tenuous ground and has never been seen as legally or morally equivalent to political speech. In recent years, however, the Court has tended to offer more substantial protection for commercial speech than it did several decades ago. According to Michael Carroll, "With the development of our information economy, the Court has come to read the First Amendment to provide broader protection over the nexus between the marketplace of ideas and the marketplace for goods and services."[20]

The potential violation of free speech rights by those who want to suppress spam is further complicated by the difficulty of deciding which communications should be classified as "spam," that is, as junk e-mail. Consider the controversial case of *Intel Corporation v. Hamidi.* Mr. Hamidi, a former Intel employee, was issued an injunction barring him from sending e-mail to Intel employees connected to the company's network. Hamidi's mail consisted of protests and complaints about Intel's poor treatment of its employees. Intel maintained, and a court agreed, that Hamidi's mass mailings were equivalent to junk commercial e-mail that disrupted its operations and distracted its employees. What makes this case difficult is the fact that Hamidi's speech was noncommercial. He was not advertising a product but rendering an opinion, however alien that opinion might have been in the Intel work environment.

A similar incident arose at a Pratt & Whitney factory in Florida, where a union organizing drive used e-mail to contact the company's 2,000 engineers to solicit their interest in joining the union. According to Noam Cohen, unions have found e-mail to be "an unusually effective organizing tool, one that combines the intimacy of a conversation, the efficiency of mass-produced leaflets and the precision of delivery by mail to work forces that are often widely dispersed."[21] But companies like Pratt & Whitney argue that these intrusive mass mailings are the same as spam and must be suppressed to avoid the negative effects of spam, such as congestion of their networks.

These and other cases suggest some provocative free speech questions. Should all bulk e-mail, even noncommercial communications, be considered spam? If the Internet is to realize its full potential as a "democratizing force," shouldn't some forms of bulk e-mail be permitted, both morally and legally? What should be the decisive factors in determining when bulk e-mail is intrusive spam or a legitimate form of communication?

What can be done about bulk e-mail that *is* classified as spam? Should it be subject to government regulations because of its deleterious side effects? Some regulatory possibilities include an outright ban on spam or a labeling requirement. The first option could be implemented by amending the Telephone Consumer Protection Act of 1991 (TCPA), which already makes it illegal to transmit unsolicited commercial advertisements over a facsimile machine. The TCPA could be modified to include unsolicited commercial e-mail as well as junk faxes. However, there would most likely be a constitutional challenge to a complete ban on spam because it appears to violate the First Amendment. Also, for those who want to preserve the Internet's libertarian ethic, it is unsettling to proscribe communications such as e-mail based purely on its content.

The second option is a labeling requirement. All unsolicited commercial e-mail and Internet advertising would have a common identifier or a label, allowing users to filter it out if they so desired. With accurate labels, ISPs could more easily control incoming spam, either by preventing any unsolicited advertising from their networks or by allowing those ads to reach only the destinations that have agreed to accept such e-mails.

Critics of the latter approach argue that if a labeling requirement were enacted, it would implicitly legitimize spam, and this could have the perverse effect of actually increasing its volume. Spam might become a more acceptable way of advertising, and this could increase the burden on consumers and ISPs to filter out even more unwanted junk e-mail.

Another solution to the problem of spam for those who oppose regulations and prefer a more bottoms-up approach is exclusive reliance on code without the support of the law. Filters are now available that will weed out spam while allowing legitimate mail to come through, even if spam is not appropriately labeled. Crude e-mail filters that look for signs of spam such as messages that contain words like "Free!" have been on the market for some time. More sophisticated filters that distinguish junk mail from real mail are also being developed. Microsoft, for example, has developed a filter that relies on a multidimensional vector space to identify junk mail. This filter examines many more variables than ordinary ones. As a result, when the Microsoft filter is deployed, "it takes a constellation of symptoms to trigger the diagnosis of spam—some having to do with the words in a message and some with its appearance (for example, a high percentage of characters like ! and $$$)."[22]

Once again, we are confronted with a choice between top-down regulations or a bottoms-up approach with fallible, yet effective, antispam technology. Of course, the same dangers that accompany the filtering of pornography could be applicable when filtering spam. Filtering protocols, even those that are well intentioned, come with a cost. As David Shapiro observes, excessive filtering "may cause our preferences to become ever more narrow and specialized, depriving us of a broad perspective when we likely need it most."[23]

## ▶ PostScript

Spam, pornography, libel, hate speech—all are problematic forms of free expression that pose formidable challenges to cyberspace jurisprudence, which seeks to balance individual rights with the public good. Ideally, of course, individuals and organizations should regulate their own expression by refraining from hate speech, refusing to disseminate pornography to children, and repressing the temptation to use spam as a means of advertising goods or services. In the absence of such self-restraint, Internet stakeholders must make difficult decisions about whether to shield themselves from unwanted speech, whether it be crude obscenities or irksome junk e-mail.

Top-down government regulations such as the CDA II or laws that ban junk e-mail represent one method for solving this problem. Sophisticated filtering devices, which will undoubtedly continue to improve in their precision and accuracy, offer a different, but more chaotic, alternative. As we have been at pains to insist here, whatever combination of constraints are used—code, law, market, or norms—full respect must be accorded to key moral values such as personal autonomy; hence the need for nuanced ethical reflection about how these universal moral standards can best be preserved as we develop effective constraints for aberrant behavior in cyberspace. Otherwise, our worst apprehensions about the tyranny of the code *or* the laws of cyberspace may be realized.

Another option, of course, is to refrain from the temptation to take *any* action against these controversial forms of speech in cyberspace. Some civil libertarians convincingly argue that Internet stakeholders should eschew regulations and filtering and leave the Internet as unfettered as possible. We should tolerate nuisance speech on the Internet just as we tolerate it in the physical world.

## Discussion Questions

1. What is your assessment of CDA II? Do you support the ACLU's views against this legislation?
2. Are automated content controls such as PICS a reasonable means of dealing with pornographic material on the Internet? At what level(s)—parents, schools/libraries, ISPs, etc.—should it occur?
3. What sort of First Amendment protection do Web sites filled with hate speech or racist speech deserve?
4. Do you agree with the position that anonymity should be preserved in cyberspace? Or should every user's digital identity be mandated in some way?

## CASE STUDY

### The Librarian's Dilemma (Hypothetical)

Assume that you have just taken over as the head librarian of a library system in a medium-size city in the United States. You discover that the main library building in the heavily populated downtown area has six Macintosh computers, but they are used only sporadically by this library's many patrons. The computers lack any interesting software and do not have Internet connectivity. As one of your first orders of business, you decide to purchase some popular software packages and to provide Internet access through Netscape's Navigator browser. The computer room soon becomes a big success. The computers are in constant use, and the most popular activity is Web surfing. You are pleased with this decision because this is an excellent way for those in the community who cannot afford computer systems to gain access to the Internet.

Soon, however, some problems begin to emerge. On one occasion, some young teenagers (probably about twelve or thirteen years old) are seen downloading graphic sexual material. A shocked staff member tells you that these young boys were looking at sadistic obscene images when they were asked to leave the library. About ten days later, an older man was noticed looking at child pornography for several hours. Every few weeks, there are similar incidents.

Your associate librarian and several other staff members recommend that you purchase and immediately install some type of filtering software. Other librarians remind you that this violates the ALA's code of responsibility. You re-read that code and are struck by the following sentence: "The selection and development of library resources should not be diluted because of minors having the same access to library resources as adult users." They urge you to resist the temptation to filter, an activity they equate with censorship. One staff member argues that filtering is equivalent to purchasing an encyclopedia and cutting out articles that do not meet certain standards. Another librarian points out that the library does not put pornographic material in its collection, so why should it allow access to such material on the Internet?

As word spreads about this problem, there is also incipient public pressure from community leaders to do something about these computers. Even the mayor has weighed in—she too is uncomfortable with unfettered access. What should you do?

### Questions

1. Is filtering of pornographic Web sites an acquisition decision or does it represent an attempt to censor the library's collection?
2. Do libraries have any legal and/or moral duty to protect children from indecent and obscene material?
3. What course of action would you take? Defend your position.

## CASE STUDY

### Spam or Free Speech at Intel?

Mr. Kenneth Hamidi is a disgruntled, former employee of Intel who has problems with the way Intel treats its workers. Hamidi is the founder and spokesperson of an organization known as FACE, a group of current and former Intel employees, many of whom claim that they have been mistreated by Intel. Hamidi was dismissed from Intel for reasons that have not been made public, but he claims to be a victim of discrimination.

Shortly after his dismissal in the fall of 1996, Hamidi began e-mailing Intel employees, informing them of Intel's unfair labor practices. He alleges that the company is guilty of widespread age and disability discrimination, but Intel firmly denies this allegation. According to Intel, Hamidi sent e-mail messages complaining about Intel's employment policies to over 30,000 employees on six occasions between 1996 and 1998. One message, for example, accused Intel of grossly underestimating the size of an impending layoff.

Intel's position was that Hamidi's bulk e-mail was the equivalent of spam, congesting its e-mail network and distracting its employees. Intel's lawyers have contended that these unsolicited mailings were intrusive and costly for the corporation. Moreover, the unwanted messages are analogous to trespass on Intel's property: just as a trespasser forces his or her way onto someone's else's property so these messages were being forced upon Intel and its employees.

In summary, their basic argument is that Hamidi does not have a right to express his personal views on Intel's proprietary e-mail system. They also point out that Hamidi has many other forums to express his opinions, such as the FACE Web site.

In November 1998, a California Superior Court judge agreed with these arguments and issued an injunction prohibiting Hamidi from sending any more bulk e-mail to Intel's employees.

Defenders of Hamidi's actions argue that the injunction is an unfair overreaction and that his free speech rights are being violated. They claim that this bulk e-mail should not be categorized as spam because it took the form of noncommercial speech, which deserves full First Amendment protection. Hamidi's speech involves ideas; it is not an attempt to sell goods or services over the Internet. Hamidi, therefore, has a First Amendment right to disseminate his e-mail messages to Intel's employees, even if the company is inconvenienced in the process.

## Questions

1. Does Hamidi's speech deserve First Amendment protection? Should he be allowed to send these messages without court interference?
2. What do you make of Intel's argument that its censoring of Hamidi's bulk e-mail amounts to protecting its private property?
3. Should there be new laws to clarify this issue? How might those laws be crafted?

## References

1. Godwin, M. 1998. *CyberRights*. New York: Random House, p. 16.
2. *ACLU v. Reno*, 521 U.S., 870 (1997).
3. *Ginsberg v. New York*, 390 U.S. 15 (1973).
4. Elmer-Dewitt, P. 1995. Cyberporn. *Time*, July 3, p. 40.
5. Godwin, M. p. 223.
6. See *Communications Decency Act*, 47 U.S.C. # 223 (d) (1) (B).
7. Zittrain et al. Brief for Appelants. *Reno v. ACLU*, no. 96-511.
8. *ACLU v. Reno*, 882.
9. Halperin, M. 1999. The COPA battle and the future of free speech. *Communications of the ACM* 42(1):25.
10. Mendels, P. 1999. Setback for a law shielding minors from smut Web sites. *The New York Times*, February 2, p. A10.
11. Katz, J. 1997.*Virtuous reality*. New York: Random House, p. 184.
12. Sunstein, C. 1995. The First Amendment in cyberspace. *Yale Law Journal* 104:1757.
13. Quoted in Harmon, A. 1997. To screen or not to screen: Libraries confront Internet access. *The New York Times*, June 23, p. D8.
14. See the American Library Association Web site, www.ala.org.
15. Rosenberg, R. 1993. Free speech, pornography, sexual harassment, and electronic networks. *The Information Society* 9:289.
16. See John Finnis' (1980) insightful discussion of these issues in *Natural law and natural rights*. Oxford: Oxford University Press, pp. 216–218.

17. Froomkin, M. 1996. Flood control on the information ocean: Living with anonymity, digital cash, and distributed data bases. *University of Pittsburgh Journal of Law and Commerce* 395:278.
18. Brin, D. 1998. *The transparent society.* Reading, MA: Addison-Wesley, p. 27.
19. Raisch, R. *Postage due marketing: An Internet company white paper.* Available at http://www.internet.com:2010/marketing/postage.html.
20. Carroll, M. 1996. Garbage in: Emerging media and regulation of unsolicited commercial solicitations. *Berkeley Technology Law Journal* 11(Fall).
21. Cohen, N. 1999. Corporations battling to bar use of e-mail for unions. *The New York Times*, August 23, p. C1.
22. Baldwin, W. 1998. Spam killers. *Forbes*, September 21, p. 255.
23. Shapiro, p. 114.

# CHAPTER FOUR

# Intellectual Property in Cyberspace

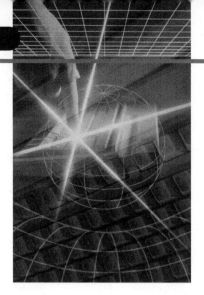

## ▼ PART I: BACKGROUND ON INTELLECTUAL PROPERTY

### ▶ Introduction

The struggle to adapt copyright and patent laws to the complex realities of the networked digital age has already been long and contentious. In December 1996, a major conference was convened in Geneva to devise an international copyright treaty. To the dismay of Bruce Lehman, the Assistant Secretary of Commerce, and the American delegation, no consensus could be reached on the major issues.

Given the precariousness of maintaining some semblance of control over one's intellectual property in cyberspace, Lehman sought stricter rules and powers of ownership for content creators, that is, record companies, book and magazine publishers, movie studios, and software vendors. Pamela Samuelson describes those who advocate this view as "copyright maximalists," and she explains that "the maximalist agenda would have given publishers rights over every temporary reproduction in computer memory (such as copies made when browsing on the Internet) and every transmission of copyrighted works in digital form; it would also have eliminated fair-use rights in the digital environment and pushed much of the cost and effort of policing copyright infringement on to on-line service providers."[1]

Clearly, the maximalist agenda flies in the face of the libertarian approach to intellectual property, which tends to de-emphasize property rights. "Information wants to be free" is a familiar refrain of some libertarians who oppose intellectual property laws that constrain the free flow of information in cyberspace.

Even some conservatives and moderates who promote strong intellectual property protection were chagrined by the imbalance of power between content users and content providers that would have been created by the new Geneva treaties. Of particular concern has been the proposed attenuation of fair use rights, which would make research and the dissemination of knowledge a more arduous task.

At the other extreme, we have the minimalist approach, which is supported by many libertarians and others who believe that trying to preserve intellectual property protection in this digital era is a futile and misguided effort. Esther Dyson for one has argued that copyright in cyberspace is an anachronism and that authors will soon be forced to give away their books on the Internet and make money through other activities (such as lectures). Others, like John Perry Barlow, have deeper philosophical reasons for opposing Internet copyright protection. He argues that ownership of information in this open environment is antidemocratic because it will interfere with the free circulation of ideas.

Can we stake out a reasonable middle ground between the maximalists and the minimalists? Or are the disagreements and divisions so deep-seated that a tenable compromise is almost impossible? Also, should fair use requirements be curtailed given the higher risk of its abuse in cyberspace?

The squabbles that dominated the Geneva conference suggest the shape of the debate over the key questions that must be considered if a reasonable middle ground is to be attained. One problem revolves around the distinction between the public and the private in cyberspace. The fair use provision of copyright law has always permitted *private* use of copyrighted material. I can photocopy a chapter from a book that is protected by copyright without breaking any laws as long as this material is for my own personal use. There is a problem, however, if I am making the copy for *public* consumption, such as for distribution to a large audience. But can we make this clear distinction in the interconnected world of cyberspace? To come to terms with this question, more fundamental ones need attention such as what constitutes a "copy" in cyberspace and who exactly is the public?

Another broad question concerns the scope of copyright protection over digital products, especially those made available on the Internet. Should it include, for example, a new form of property right in the content of databases? For example, should a company be able to copyright a database of financial information that has been costly to create? If not, what will stop someone else from downloading this data and reselling it? This too was a proposal advanced by the United States in Geneva. If these new protections are implemented, who should be responsible for enforcement? Should on-line service providers be held liable for copyright infringements that occur among their users?

The vexing nature of these questions perhaps accounts for why so little was accomplished at the Geneva meeting. Only when these questions are debated and more properly addressed can we come to terms with the normative issues that are the key to achieving the right balance between the needs of the purveyors and the users of digital information.

There are a host of other novel intellectual property issues triggered by expanded use of the Internet and the emergence of Web sites. Do organizations have property rights in domain names (for example, www.cocacola. com) once they are properly registered, and what is the precise scope of those rights? How do we control and restrict the use of meta tags in Web sites? What is the fairest approach to framing and linking to other Web sites? Does linking to another Web site ever infringe on intellectual property rights? Also, do copyright and trademark owners have the prerogative to restrict the use of their work on the Internet? Are the creators of the now infamous "Distorted Barbie" (a Web art Barbie doll image) merely exercising creative license or infringing on Mattel's property rights?

In this chapter, we provide some perspective on all of these matters, primarily from a moral vantage point. It seems fitting that we begin by explaining why intellectual property protection is still important for certain kinds of material. In the context of that discussion, we also provide an overview of the framework of relevant laws that protect intellectual property along with an account of the most plausible moral grounding of those laws. In addition, keeping in mind the "Lessig framework" introduced in the first chapter, we must consider what combinations of law and code are most appropriate to effectively regulate property in cyberspace without undermining fair use. Software code is coming that will give content providers much more control over their material, but is this also a case where the cure may be worse than the disease?

## ▶ What Is Intellectual Property and Why Does It Matter?

### A Definition of Property

It is instructive to begin this analysis by considering briefly a workable definition of *property* and an overview of its central role in a well-ordered society. Property is at the cornerstone of most legal systems, yet it is a murky and complex concept that defies a simple definition.

Most contemporary philosophical analyses equate the notions of "ownership" and "property." Hence, the statements "I own that house," and "That house is my property," are equivalent because they convey the same information. Furthermore, those analyses define ownership as "the greatest possible interest in a thing which a mature system of law recognizes."[2] More simply, ownership of property implies that the owner has certain rights and liabilities with respect to this property, including the rights to use, manage, possess, exclude, and derive income. This is consistent with our legal tradition, which has long recognized that ownership encompasses a number of rights known as the *Blackstonian Bundle,* named after William Blackstone, who summarized these rights in his famous eighteenth century *Commentaries.* According to Blackstone, the owner has the right to exclude anyone from the property, to use it as he or she sees fit, to receive income derived from that property, or to transfer the property to someone else.

Why do property rights matter so much? The principles of justice, economic efficiency, and political freedom have been invoked to defend the basic structure of property rights. In a recent book on this topic called *Property Matters,* James DeLong observes that unless we have unambiguous ownership rights and unless we pay for the goods (that is, property) that we need, the result will be greed and chaos: "If you must pay, then it forces thought about what is really valuable and what is not. If the property is free the outcome is obvious: take everything you can get your hands on."[3] The abuse of free goods, such as land, air, and water, has already led to serious environmental degradation and a "tragedy of the commons." Similar tragedies could arise if property rights are diluted and ownership shifts too dramatically from the private to the common. It is somewhat different with intangible intellectual property, but there are some important analogies: personal data sold and exchanged by data brokers can also be abused because it has become such a cheap commodity.

## Intellectual Property

Intellectual property consists of "intellectual objects," such as original musical compositions, poems, novels, inventions, product formulas, and so forth. Although the use of physical objects is a zero-sum game in the sense that my use of an object prohibits others from using it, the same cannot be said of intellectual objects. They are nonexclusive because they can be used by many people simultaneously and their use by some does not preclude their use by others. My appropriation of a special recipe for pasta primavera does not preclude others from enjoying that same recipe. Furthermore, although the development of intellectual property objects may be time-consuming and costly, the marginal cost of providing additional access to intellectual property is usually negligible.

All of these characteristics make intellectual property rights more difficult to define and justify, especially in open, democratic societies that prize free expression and the free flow of ideas. Assigning property rights to intellectual objects seems antithetical to many of the goals and traditions of a free society. Thus, those who oppose strong copyright protections often appeal to the First Amendment, along with the need for maximum vitality in the marketplace of ideas as a rationale for their opposition.

Nonetheless, for reasons that will become more lucid as this chapter proceeds, limited property rights should extend to the intellectual realm. Like physical property rights, intellectual property rights imply that someone has the right to certain concepts, knowledge, or information. But there are obvious difficulties with the notion that one has property rights in an idea because this would mean the "right" to exclude others from using and building upon those ideas. This problem is overcome by making a distinction between the idea and its expression and, in most cases, granting copyright protection to the expression of an idea but not the idea itself.

## ▶ Legal Protection for Intellectual Property

Intellectual property objects that are most at risk in cyberspace are usually protected in one of these three ways: (1) copyrights, (2) patents, and (3) trademarks.

### Trademarks

The first form of legal protection for intellectual property objects is the trademark, which is a word, phrase, or symbol that pithily identifies a product or service. Examples abound: the Nike "swoosh" symbol, names like *Pepsi* and *Dr. Pepper*, and logos such as the famous bitten apple image crafted by Apple Computer. To qualify as a trademark, the mark or name must be truly distinctive. In legal terms, distinctiveness is determined by several factors, including the following: is the trademark "arbitrary or fanciful," that is, not logically connected to the product (e.g., the Apple Computer logo has no connection to a computer); and is the trademark powerfully descriptive or suggestive in some way?

A trademark is acquired when someone is either the first to use the mark publicly or registers it with the U.S. Patent Office. Trademarks do not necessarily last in perpetuity. They can be lost if one squanders a trademark through excessive or improper licensing. They can also become lost if they eventually become generic and thereby enter the public domain.

Trademarks are generally violated in one of two ways: they can be infringed upon, or they can be diluted. Infringement occurs when the trademark is used by someone else in connection with the sale of its goods or services. If an upstart athletic shoe company tried to sell its products with the aid of the "swoosh" symbol, it would be violating Nike's trademark.

The general standard for infringement is the likelihood of consumer confusion. Trademark owners can also bring forth legal claims if their trademarks are diluted. Dilution is applicable only to famous trademarks that are distinctive, of long duration, and usually known to the public through extensive advertising and publicity. Dilution is the result of either "blurring" or "tarnishment." Blurring occurs when the trademark is associated with dissimilar products, for example, using the Disney trademark name to sell suits for men. Tarnishment occurs when the mark is portrayed in a negative or compromising way or associated with products or services of questionable value or reputation.

Trademark law allows for fair use of trademarks and also use for purposes of parody. In fair use situations, the trademark name normally assumes its primary (versus commercial) meaning; for example, describing a cereal as comprised of "all bran" is different from infringing on the Kellog's brand name "All Bran." Parody of trademarks is permitted as long as it is not closely connected with commercial use. Making fun of a well-known brand in a Hollywood skit is probably acceptable, but parodying that brand to sell a competing product would most likely not be allowed.[4]

## Patents

A patent is generally awarded for a period of seventeen years. The federal government has established a fairly broad standard for products that fall under patency protection. According to the U.S. Code on patents,

> Whoever invents or discovers any new and useful process, machine, manufacture, or composition of matter, or any new and useful improvement thereof, may obtain a patent.[5]

Thus, the primary candidates for patent protection are original, useful, and "nonobvious" inventions, such as machines and processes or compositions of matter such as a new pharmaceutical product. Formulas, scientific principles, and so on belong in the public domain and cannot be patented.

There has actually been a prolonged legal debate over whether software programs and the algorithms that they incorporate should be eligible for patent protection. In the 1972 decision *Gottschalk v. Benson*, the Supreme Court ruled that such algorithms were unpatentable. However, this ruling was reversed in the 1981 landmark case *Diamond v. Diehr*, when the Court ruled that a patent claim for a process should not be rejected merely because it includes a mathematical algorithm or computer program. In this case, "the majority opinion of the Court concluded Diehr's process to be nothing more than a process for molding rubber products and not an attempt to patent a mathematical formula."[6] In other words, the process itself (in this case one for curing rubber) must be original and hence patentable, and if computer calculations are part of the process, then they are included in the patent protection.

Patents have been the subject of some scorn and criticism in certain industries. Because patents give one a monopoly power over the product or invention, they enable the producer to charge high prices and reap monopoly rents. This has been a serious source of contention for breakthrough pharmaceutical products, which are often unavailable to indigent patients as a result of monopoly pricing practices. Patent protection seems anticompetitive, but without it, would companies have the incentive to invest millions of dollars to invent breakthrough drugs or other innovations? The assumption in the Anglo-American capitalist system is that by creating powerful incentives for companies and individuals that take the form of strongly protected monopolies for their innovations, there will be a greater number of breakthrough inventions that will benefit society in the long run.

The emergence of innovative commercial enterprises on the Web has triggered some novel patent controversies. The U.S. Patent Office has been awarding patents that enable vendors to protect their business models from imitators. Priceline.comLLC, Inc., for instance, was awarded a patent for its Web-based business that sells airline tickets and awards customers frequent flyer miles on their Internet purchases. This type of patent is controversial because it applies to such general business models and may end up precluding legitimate competition. It may also lead to an overflow of vendors applying for regulatory patent protection. The real problem is that attention could be diverted from creating new cyberspace products to worrying about the possibility of inadvertently stealing a competitor's "patented" idea.

## Copyright Laws

The third and final form of protection for intellectual property are the copyright laws. Copyrights are easier to obtain than patents and have a much longer duration (they last for an author's lifetime plus seventy years). Copyright protects a literary, musical, dramatic, artistic, architectural, audio, or audiovisual work from being reproduced without the permission of the copyright holder. To be eligible for copyright protection, the work in question must be original; that is, it must be independently created by its author. The work must also be embodied in some tangible medium of expression. Thus, a dance itself cannot be copyrighted, but a visual recording of that dance would be eligible for copyright protection. Also, it is important to underscore that copyright protection extends to the actual concrete expression of an idea but not to the idea itself. Copyright laws do not protect ideas, concepts, principles, algorithms, and so forth.

As we observed at the beginning of this chapter, copyright laws permit "fair use" of these creative works, which can be cited for educational or critical purposes. The fair use provision of the copyright law allows for the reproduction and use of a work for limited purposes, including criticism, research, and classroom instruction. There are limits, albeit ambiguous ones, on how much of a work can be reproduced. Fair use would enable a teacher to reproduce and distribute a few paragraphs from a book or magazine article, but it would probably not allow reproduction of the whole article or several chapters of the book.

In the 1970s, when the software industry was in its infancy, there was much debate over whether software qualified to come under copyright protection. But in 1980, an amendment to the 1976 Copyright Act gave software developers the same protection enjoyed by other authors, such as novelists and movie script writers. This amendment stipulated that federal copyright laws protect not only source code (the lines of computer code written by programmers in a high-level language such as JAVA, BASIC, or C) but also the object code (the binary code created when the source code is compiled). Broader protection for the logic and design of a proprietary program has been a matter of some dispute.

Thus, copyright infringement of software could occur in many different ways. An individual or organization could appropriate the source code of a competitor's program and sell that program as one's own creation. Such direct cloning, especially through a misappropriation of source code, would clearly violate copyright laws. Someone could also make duplicate copies of the finished product instead of purchasing or licensing their own copy. For example, if one buys a word processing program for one's personal computer and lends the disk out so that it can be copied by friends and colleagues in violation of the licensing agreement, the copyright laws have also been broken.

## ▶ Moral Justifications for Intellectual Property

We have considered the various forms of legal protection for intellectual property, but is there a philosophical and moral justification for these laws? Certainly, many theories of property have been put forth, and some of these theories can be used to provide a tenable justification of intellectual property law. Two of the most pertinent justifications can be found in the philosophies of John Locke and G.W.F. Hegel. Locke's labor theory of value has commonly been invoked to defend rights to physical property and these arguments can also be applied to intellectual property. We can also supplement Locke's theory with a personality justification for intellectual property found in the work of Hegel.

Locke's theory of property has undoubtedly been one of the most influential in the entire tradition. Stripped of its subtleties, his thesis is simple enough: people have a natural right or entitlement to the fruits of their labor. Thus, if someone takes common, unusable land and through the sweat of the brow transforms it into valuable farm land, that person deserves to own that land. Locke's basic argument is that labor is an unpleasant and onerous activity and therefore people do it only to reap its benefits; as a result, it would be unjust not to let people have these benefits they take such pains to procure. In short, property rights are required as a return for the laborers' painful and strenuous work.

There are numerous problems with Locke's theory, such as the assumption of plenitude. Also, it seems outdated and irrelevant. We do not mix labor with nature but with a complex economic system; a person's labor is only a small input contributing to the production of goods. Nonetheless, the theory does contain a kernel of truth: people ought to receive a just reward for their labor, and when nothing but a property right will be adequate compensation, they should be entitled to that right.

In making the case for property rights, Locke clearly had in mind tangible property, but can his arguments be applied to intellectual property? Because the production of most ideas and other intellectual objects most often requires some intense labor, Locke's justification seems to have some relevance. It follows from Locke's main argument that because the pain and difficulty of physical labor should be rewarded with property, likewise the difficulty and arduousness of mental effort and creative work should also be so rewarded. It is assumed that because all labor is a disutility, a significant reward is necessary to provide an incentive to overcome that disutility.

In some cases, however, labor is not a disutility; specifically, the production and expression of ideas may not be so arduous or unpleasant. But as Justin Hughes points out, there is another interpretation of Locke's labor justification called the *value-added* theory. This is a consequentialist argument stipulating that "people will add value to the common if some of the added value accrues to them personally."[7] Individuals should be rewarded for the value they add to society and the lives of others, regardless of the pleasantness or unpleasantness of the effort involved.

Thus, because of the effort involved *and* the value created, when an individual creates an original work and expresses it in some concrete medium, that individual ought to have a property right in this work, provided that others are not made worse off. The proviso that individuals can improve their position as long as the position of others is not worsened is consistent with Locke's caveat that when property is appropriated there is "enough and as good left for others."

We are still left with one problem if we want to rely exclusively on a Lockean justification of intellectual property. What if an idea or mental product involves little or no labor? Locke's theory assuredly cannot account for this, and hence the need to supplement this justification with an additional theory that can account for these rare situations. Hughes presents a compelling case that Hegel's personality justification can serve this purpose.

Hegel argued that property was necessary for the realization of freedom, as individuals put their personality into the world. According to Reeve, "Property enables an individual to put his [or her] will into a 'thing.'"[8] Property then is an expression of personality. As human beings freely externalize their will in various things, such as novels, works of art, craftsmanship, or even more mundane objects, they create property to which they are entitled because it is an expression of who they are. It is an extension of their being and as such belongs to them.

These arguments have even more force when applied to intellectual objects, which are clearly an expression of the author's personality. Shouldn't the author have a right to control his or her individual expression, to prevent its misappropriation and misuse? If I write a poem expressing my innermost feelings, that poem is a part of me and I should have the right to control its use, that is, the specifics of how it is shared with others. Thus, even if the creation of intellectual property entails little or no labor, Hegel's conception of property provides a rationale for why the end product should belong to its creator. We might summarize this argument for intellectual property rights as follows:

> (i) Laborers are entitled to the fruits of their intellectual labor since labor is a disutility.
>
> (ii) Even if labor is not a disutility, the laborer deserves this reward since his/her work adds value, and the incentive to add value is greatly enhanced if some of that value accrues to the laborer personally.
>
> (iii) If works are created with little or no labor the creator should still have ownership rights since these works represent an expression of the laborer's personality, and to resign these works completely to the common domain violates the right to control one's individual expression since the works can be subject to abuse.

We do not need to rely on the philosophies of Locke and Hegel for a justification of intellectual property rights. One can also make a strong case for these rights for more pragmatic, utilitarian reasons. Despite the costs associated with assigning these rights, there are two major benefits of great significance: limited property rights are an essential way (1) to *reward* one's past creation, regardless of the labor involved, and (2) to provide *incentives* to create or produce in the future. The primary cost is the impediment that property rights create for the free flow of ideas and knowledge. But without the proper incentives, good ideas and worthwhile information may be in short supply. Books may not be written, music may not be recorded, and perhaps even some masterpieces may not be conceived—unless creators can be assured of some reward for their effort.

Although Locke's labor-desert argument or utilitarian reasoning has often been invoked to provide a rationale for intellectual property, James Boyle argues that the real justification is rooted in our overly romanticized notion of "authorship." Society sees the author as an original creator who crafts something new. By granting this new work some protection, we can justly reward its author and set that work apart from the public domain. Because this work is new, this protection will not diminish the common stock of knowledge and ideas. According to Boyle, "it is the *originality* of the author, the novelty which he or she adds to the raw materials provided by culture and the common pool which 'justifies' the property right."[9]

This romantic figure of the author and the theme of originality serve as the underlying justification of intellectual property rights. But the right is qualified by the important idea/expression distinction, which is supposed to resolve the tensions between the need for protection and the need to preserve our common reservoir of knowledge. Hence, according to Boyle's framework, these three themes (the romantic author figure, originality, and preserving the idea/expression dichotomy) shape our legal infrastructure on copyright protection.

Moreover, this "author vision" has induced us to be overzealous in our efforts at intellectual property protection and to privatize intellectual goods that ought to remain in the public domain. The Clinton Administration's 1995 White Paper on intellectual property rights on the Internet tends to confirm this trend. This controversial White Paper articulated legitimate concerns about how ease of access on the Internet would facilitate illegitimate copying. It proposed the curtailment of fair use and even planned to put restrictions on the ability to read documents with a browser. The presumption was that cyberspace warranted even tighter protections than real space.

Although most of the proposals in the White Paper have not yet materialized, the recent passage of the Sonny Bono Copyright Term Extension Act of 1998 (CTEA) may be a portent of things to come. This Act essentially adds another twenty years to the term of most copyrights. Under the copyright law passed in 1976, copyright protection lasted for fifty years after the author's death, but this will now be extended to seventy years. In the case of corporate authors (such as Paramount Pictures), the copyright term for works published before 1978 was seventy-five years. Something published in 1923 by a corporate author would have been scheduled to enter the public domain in 1998, but now that will not happen until 2018. The American film industry, along with heirs to copyright owners, lobbied heavily for passage of this bill.

Clearly, as Boyle and others have predicted, the public domain seems to be losing out in favor of more substantial protection for authors. However, if countries like the United States are too overprotective of their information resources, they run the risk of depleting the common pool of knowledge along with those seminal ideas that are the building blocks for future creative projects.[10]

# ▼ PART II: ISSUES FOR THE INTERNET

## ▶ Digital Rights Architectures

Throughout this chapter, we have expressed how difficult it is for intellectual property laws to keep pace with the power and capabilities of the Internet. As more and more people gain access to electronic distribution, intellectual property is being devalued through illicit copying in cyberspace. Therefore, it is no surprise that code and technology may soon supplant the law as the driving force of regulation. The law has sought to balance the public interest of sharing knowledge with the private interest of content providers, but "code" may work more to the advantage of private interests and therefore dramatically shift that balance.

One prominent digital rights management technology that is giving content providers enhanced control over their material is called a *trusted system*. A trusted system consists of hardware and software that is programmed to follow certain rules or usage rights that express how and when a digital work can be used. According to Mark Stefik, "trusted systems can take different forms, such as trusted readers for viewing digital books, trusted players for playing audio and video recordings, trusted printers for making copies that contain labels (watermarks) that denote copyright status, and trusted servers that sell digital works on the Internet."[11] Content providers would distribute their work in cyberspace in encrypted form in such a manner that they would be accessible only by users with trusted machines. An elaborate rule system would incorporate the fees and conditions associated with particular works, and these rules would be deciphered by the trusted system. For example, if I wanted to buy a record album on-line, a trusted player would enable me to play but not reproduce the music so long as the proper on-line payment was rendered to the record company.

Although the trusted system approach may seem like an ideal solution to the problem of intellectual property protection on the Internet, it also poses some unique challenges. How would fair use coexist with trusted systems? Would critics, scholars, and teachers need to go through elaborate mechanisms to access their material? Furthermore, these systems enable content providers to choose who will access their material, and it is possible that certain groups might be excluded from viewing or listening to certain material. If trusted systems are not constructed properly, they could eviscerate the fair use provisions of copyright laws and make creative works less accessible to the general public.

Another grave problem with trusted systems is the potential for invasions of privacy. These systems will allow content creators to keep precise tabs on who is accessing and purchasing their material. This raises the Orwellian spectre of demands for this information from lawyers, government officials, or other curious third parties. Do we really want anyone to keep tabs on which books we read or what kind of record albums we purchase?

It seems evident that trusted systems have the potential to change the ground rules for intellectual property protection. Code can be far more efficacious than law in guarding against infringement. But what will be the cost to other valuable social goods such as fair use and personal privacy?

Trusted systems provide yet another vivid example of Lessig's point that code can be more powerful and comprehensive than law in regulating the Internet. Code allows for almost perfect and foolproof control that is beyond the capability of a more fallible legal system. In effect, the code threatens to privatize copyright law, without the appropriate checks and balances we find in public copyright law.

If trusted systems do become popular, it may be necessary for government to intercede to protect fair use. Perhaps the right combination of reasonable laws that keep in mind the public good and the code, which is more slanted to the private good of personal control, might work and produce a superior copyright system. For example, laws could require that trusted systems permit fair use access to students, teachers, and researchers and that they do not discriminate among users. Other incentives could also be instantiated in the law to encourage fair use. Code is private law, and like the public law of copyright, there must be clear limits to the intellectual property rights that are inscribed in that code.

Furthermore, recall that in the enhancement of Lessig's framework, we added a fifth constraint, common ethical standards, which cannot be bracketed by those who develop code or write laws. This would imply that the developers and users of trusted systems must respect the value of privacy, which is a basic human right (see Chapter Five). Trusted systems must incorporate rules that protect and do not undermine personal privacy. In this case, what must be safeguarded is the right to read, view, or listen to copyrighted works anonymously, without the fear that one's aesthetic tastes will be used against one in a legal proceeding or a job search. If ethical standards are included in this complex equation, trusted systems may indeed be part of a workable solution to the formidable challenge of intellectual property protection.

## ▶ The Future of Software Ownership

Software is a special form of intellectual property that can be protected by a patent or copyright. It can also be classified as a trade secret, but reliance on this weaker form of protection would be too risky. Software is different from other forms of intellectual property; it does not neatly fit under either legal framework. Its source code resembles a literary work that deserves copyright protection, but unlike other literary works, it has a functional nature. It resembles a "machine," which seems to mean patent protection is more suitable. However, there are certain asymmetries between software and machines such as the user interface. Is that interface also eligible for patent protection? Furthermore, what accommodations would be made for distributing software in cyberspace? Software has been especially vulnerable to piracy, and the Internet clearly increases its vulnerability.

Some argue that given its origins and unusual nature, software should not be eligible for strong copyright or patent protection. Richard Stallman, President of the Free Software Foundation, has argued with great insistence that all software should be free. Stallman claims that ownership of software programs is obstructive and counterproductive. Hence, software should be in the public domain, freely available to anyone who wants to use it, modify it, or customize it. He regards software licensing fees as an enormous disincentive to use programs because it obviously excludes many worthy users from enjoying the use of many popular programs. Ownership also interferes with the evolution and incremental improvement of software products. According to Stallman,

> Software development used to be an evolutionary process, where a person would take a program and rewrite parts of it for one new feature, and then another person would rewrite parts to add another feature; this could continue over a period of twenty years. . . . The existence of owners prevents this kind of evolution, making it necessary to start from scratch when developing a program.[12]

Stallman concludes that because the ownership of programs is so obstructive and yields such negative consequences, this practice should be abolished.

This way of thinking has apparently led some to engage in piracy to promote the goal of widespread software availability. For example, in March 1994, an MIT student, David LaMacchia, was charged with computer fraud for operating a computer bulletin board on the Internet called CYNOSURE, which distributed copies of various copyrighted software programs. LaMacchia was not accused of actually uploading or downloading any of the programs, and he did not collect any money or materially profit from this activity in any way. Although many were quick to condemn LaMacchia's efforts to act like Robin Hood in cyberspace, some legal scholars urged caution because an indictment might chill the transmission of information in cyberspace.

Thanks in part to Stallman's efforts, many Internet stakeholders have begun to reassess the propriety and utility of software ownership. As a result, the *open source* movement has gained momentum. Open-source software is different from free software because the latter does not necessarily provide access to source code. Most open-source software packages are free, but *open source* means that the program's original source code is available to anyone who wants it. It usually implies that users can redistribute that software at no charge; however, this is not always the case.

During the past few years, there has been a noticeable trend among major software vendors to make their code more openly accessible on the Internet. In 1998, Netscape surprised the software industry when it released the source code for its Navigator Web browser. In addition, the open-source code movement has been energized by the limited success of programs such as PERL and the LINUX operating system, a variation of UNIX that runs on personal computers. Any user can download LINUX free of charge. LINUX was written by Linus Torvalds when he was an undergraduate at the University of Helsinki. It is quickly becoming a feasible alternative for UNIX and other proprietary operating systems.

Open-source code software gives computer users direct access to the software's source code, enabling them to fix bugs or develop incremental enhancements. The premise is that the collective programming wisdom available on the Internet will help create software that is of better quality than any single individual or group of individuals in a company could construct.

In a highly influential essay titled "The Cathedral and the Bazaar," Eric Raymond illustrates why a dispersed group of hackers and programmers working independently ("the bazaar") can develop higher-quality software than a more cohesive group of professional, high-paid programmers employed by companies such as Microsoft or Oracle ("the cathedral"). The former approach is far superior because it can tap into the decentralized intelligence of many talented individuals loosely connected to a program by means of the Internet. The core difference underlying the cathedral versus bazaar approach is the latter's capacity for finding and fixing bugs more rapidly. According to Raymond,

> In the cathedral-builder view of programming, bugs and development problems are tricky, insidious, deep phenomena. It takes months of scrutiny by a dedicated few to develop confidence that you've wrinkled them all out. Thus the long release intervals, and the inevitable disappointment when long-awaited releases are not perfect.
>
> In the bazaar view, on the other hand, you assume that bugs are generally shallow phenomena—or, at least, that they turn shallow pretty quick when

exposed to a thousand eager co-developers pounding on every single new release. Accordingly you release more often in order to get more corrections, and as a beneficial side effect you have less to lose if an occasional botch gets out the door.[13]

The open-source code trend is likely to intensify only if software companies can make their money from software services and support rather than through the sale of the software. One benefit to vendors should be decreasing labor costs. According to Andrew Leonard, "There's never been a more cost-effective way to contract out services than to use this type of free labor."[14] Open-source software represents a new business model that may be risky and yet highly effective for both vendors and users. It promises to make software less expensive, more versatile, and more customizable, and all of these features will greatly please many frustrated software users.

The benefits of the open code approach are beyond dispute, but one problem is that it could create a dangerous free-for-all in the exchange of software programs. The current system of ownership and licensing agreements allows the creators of software to maintain control and integrity over their systems. The lines of accountability and responsibility are unambiguous. However, this would change if proprietary software systems became the equivalent of common property. Products that are modified by unqualified programmers and redistributed could contain serious flaws and problems, and it would be exceedingly difficult to assign blame and liability. Another drawback is security. A hacker could potentially insert dangerous code into an open-source product that gets redistributed to unsuspecting users.

Furthermore, this open framework for the Internet supported by the open code movement could have major implications for how the Internet will be regulated in the future. When software code is proprietary (that is, the legal property of a particular vendor, such as IBM or Apple), it can be regulated more easily by the state. Open code defies such regulation and control because users can substitute their own routines or lines of code in a particular program. Without a fixed code controlled at a single source, it becomes impossible to set a standard of protocols or routines that software program should or should not contain. If, for example, the state insisted that the code for all Internet browsers include a routine that would automatically calculate and collect a federal tax for certain Internet purchases, this regulation would be difficult to enforce if the browser code is customizable by programmers all over cyberspace. Thus, depending on one's views on government regulation, open code is either a liberating or subversive force in the struggle for sovereignty between the individual and the state.

Despite the growing enthusiasm for open and free source code, many companies, like Microsoft, will still choose to protect their software products and to tightly control distribution. It should be apparent, however, that none of the forms of intellectual property protection described thus far (copyrights and patents) are especially well suited for software. The source code of software written in languages such as C++ or JAVA is a literary creation, but software is also functional, and because of its functionality, it is inconsistent with copyright law. But does this utilitarian feature imply that patent protection is more appropriate? It does not quite fit under patent protection either because in addition to behaving as a machine, it is also an expressive literary work. Also, although software may be innovative, it is not really *inventive*. The problem, of course, is that software is both useful and literary; it is a machine, and yet it is also expressive like a work of art.

As Pamela Samuelson and her co-authors have observed, software programs "bear much of their know-how on and near their face," and this know-how is "vulnerable to copying."[15] It is well known that Steve Jobs, co-founder of Apple, first saw a graphical user interface in a Xerox research laboratory. For someone with imagination and technical acumen, creating that interface in original source code is not a problem. She goes on to explain that if the primary value of software is useful behavior, copyright law is not the proper protective mechanism because it does not protect useful behavior. In addition, if most software is really more innovative than inventive, it should not be eligible for a patent.

It therefore follows that software really needs a unique form of legal protection, probably some hybrid of patent and copyright law that considers the special characteristics of software. Samuelson suggests a new framework that protects "the sources of value" in software: the literal source code, the useful behavior produced by that code, the know-how embodied in the program, and the program's overall design. Yet any new framework should also encourage future innovative software programs. Accordingly, Samuelson proposes the following framework:

- Traditional copyright protection for the literal source code

- Protection against behavior clones for a "market-preserving period"

- Registration of innovative capabilities to encourage knowledge sharing

- Menu of "off-the-shelf liability principles and standard licenses"

The market preserving period will allow innovators to recoup their investment, and it will vary depending on the specific segment of the software industry in which the product competes. In general, this period will be much shorter than the seventeen years currently granted for patents. This new framework needs more elaboration but does represent a reasonable direction for regulating this unusual form of intellectual property.

It appears to strike the right equilibrium between the need to promote innovation and competition and the need to reward those innovators for their substantial investments.

## ▶ Ownership of Domain Names

Every Internet Web site is identified by a unique domain name, such as www.disney.com. A domain name is equivalent to a telephone number or an electronic address. They are distributed by a company, called Network Solutions, on a first-come, first-served basis for a fee. In the year 2000, the distribution of domain names will be handed over to a nonprofit organization known as ICANN (see Chapter Two).

As one would expect, there have already been numerous domain name disputes. One of the problems that has commonly arisen is known as the "twins" phenomenon, where two parties have a legitimate claim to the same name. Two years ago, Hasbro Inc. prevailed in a legal dispute against Internet Entertainment Group (IEG) in its efforts to lay claim to www.candyland.com. This domain name was first secured by IEG when Web sites were relatively novel and not widely used by private industries. Hasbro holds a trademark on this famous children's board game and maintained that IEG's Web site of the same name, which featured pornographic material, was a clear case of trademark dilution.

The second major problem is caused by "parasites." Parasites operate by registering a name similar to a famous name in order to piggyback on its allure and recognition. For example, someone might try to register a domain name such as www.disney'sgreat.com in order to take commercial advantage of Disney's valuable brand name by luring unsuspecting users, who believe that it has an official affiliation with Disney, to this Web site.

The third related problem area involves "cybersquatters," who register numerous Internet addresses in order to resell them to companies that have a claim to that same address. One resourceful cybersquatter registered domain names based on the names of major investment banks, such as jpmorganonline.com. Some of these banks paid thousands of dollars to reclaim these names.

The issues generated by these domain name controversies tend to entail complex legal nuances that center on trademark infringement. There are conflicting legal rights at stake here, especially between legitimate claims of trademark owners and the free speech rights of domain name owners. Should trademarks and their derivative domain names always hold sway in cyberspace? If so, what are the implications of such a policy?

The primary moral issue centers once again around the conflict between free speech and property rights in cyberspace. Some argue that what companies label as "parasitic behavior" or cybersquatting is an important form of free speech. The issues are complicated, but we can begin to sort them out by the examination of two case studies. Consider, for example, the Web site called www.scientology-kills.net, which carries some trenchant criticism of the scientology movement and peddles T-shirts with the same epithet. Scientology has sued this Colorado Web site owner for trademark violation, claiming that this domain name "dilutes the distinctiveness of the mark," which could "tarnish the reputation of the owner."[16] The free speech issue at stake is whether the domain name *itself* expresses a viewpoint or opinion. In this case, does "scientology-kills.net" constitute an editorial comment about scientology that should not be suppressed?

The entangled normative and legal issues in this case are difficult to sort out. The legal issue is trademark dilution, but whether this amounts to dilution is a matter of some debate. Should domain names be allowed to express an opinion as long as they do not deceive or mislead their visitors? Is this a reasonable place to draw the line in these disputes?

A strong case can be made that suppressing the "scientology kills" Web site would set a dangerous precedent. The domain name is becoming a medium for expressing one's opinions, and this should be acceptable as long as one does so within certain parameters, that is, without being deceptive, without being defamatory, and without seeking commercial gains by the unfair leveraging of another's trademark. The Web site in question is making an observation that Scientology is a dangerous movement; it is an inflammatory remark expressing a debatable and controversial opinion, but it appears to be within the bounds of one's right to free expression. As we strive to protect speech on the Internet, we must not overprotect it by using trademark laws to suppress another's critical point of view.

To be sure, a trademark is an important property right, a valuable social good that should not be subject to irresponsible dilution. This is one side of the moral equation. But on the other side is the normative starting point of the First Amendment right to free speech. Arguably, a Web site that is (1) not deceiving visitors or seeking commercial gain through its parody or adaptation of a trademark and (2) responsibly expressing an opinion without defamation should be allowed to use trademarked names like "scientology" as part of a domain name that expresses an idea or particular viewpoint. There may be cases where dilution is so material that it does become morally relevant, and those cases must be judged accordingly; however, overall the common interest would seem to be served by giving the benefit of the doubt in these disputes to the weightier claim of free speech.

In a different case, Mr. Steve Brodsky, an orthodox Jew from New Jersey, established a Web site called www.jewsforjesus.org. The site had no affiliation with the Jews for Jesus movement, which embraces Jesus as the Messiah and seeks to convert Jews to Christianity. This site, however, proclaimed the following message: "The answers you seek are already within your faith." It also provided a link to a site called Jewish Outreach, which reinforced the theological principles of the Jewish faith. The Jews for Jesus organization, whose actual Web site has the domain name www. jews-for-jesus.org, sued for trademark infringement and won the case.

Although this is similar to the scientology domain name case, it has some new wrinkles and it is fraught with a certain degree of moral ambiguity. In the scientology case, there was no allegation that the domain name itself was deceptive. But according to the Jews for Jesus organization, Brodsky's domain name was blatantly deceptive and had undoubtedly been chosen for the sole purpose of intercepting those looking for the legitimate Web site of Jews for Jesus. They maintained that this was akin to false advertising because Brodsky was representing a site as something that it wasn't. Defenders of Brodsky argue that his use of this domain name should be protected by the First Amendment. Brodsky is not selling a product or a service, but expressing an idea. They contend that in this case, trademark law is being invoked to quash free expression. However, the free speech defense seems weaker in this case because Brodsky's domain name does not express a clear opinion in the same way that the scientology domain name does.

These two cases are representative of the many disputes that will continue to arise as users stake out property rights in their domain names and apply to the state or organizations like ICANN for regulatory privilege and protection. Sorting out these disputes over legitimate rights to domain names will require refined moral and legal reasoning.

## ▶ Linking and Framing

A related controversial practice that has many implications for property rights is called *linking*. Linking, which has become ubiquitous in cyberspace, refers to the common practice of using highlighted hyperlinks within Web pages. These hyperlinks connect users to other Web pages with the click of a mouse. This is one of the most beneficial features of the Internet because it greatly facilitates on-line research and increases the ability of users to navigate the diffuse offerings on the Web. But should Web page authors have an unrestricted right to link to other Web pages? When does linking violate copyright laws and thereby infringe on property rights? And when should it offend our moral sensibility?

Some of the problems associated with freewheeling Internet linking surfaced in the *Ticketmaster v. Microsoft* case of 1997. Ticketmaster sued Microsoft, claiming that the "Seattle Sidewalk" guide on Microsoft's Web site provided links that infringed its trademark because it "circumvented the beginning pages of Ticketmaster's Web site, which displays advertisements, products, and services of entities with which Ticketmaster contracts, and have linked directly to the subsidiary pages of the Web site."[17] In other words, Ticketmaster did not necessarily object to the link itself; rather, it protested the way the link was done because it bypassed the home page and went directly to a subsidiary page within the Ticketmaster Web site. This practice has become known as "deep linking." According to one analysis, "this case raises the question of whether site proprietors may dictate to others how and where to link their pages."[18]

From a legal standpoint, it can be argued with some plausibility that the trademark infringement allegation has some merit. Linking to a position within a Web site and bypassing the home page may convey to the casual user that there is one site instead of two because it may give the impression of being a seamless whole. There could therefore be some blurring of the property lines in the consumer's mind.

Aside from the legal questions, there are more transcendent normative questions—should there be an absolute right to link on the Internet? Those who support this position maintain that a link is merely a convenient pointer to another site, to information that is publicly available on the Internet. They also contend that putting a Web site on-line constitutes implicit permission to allow links from other Web sites.

However, the position that Web site authors have an inherent right to link to any other Web site in any manner possible may go too far. To begin with, a hyperlink is more than a pointer because activating the link actually delivers the linked Web page to one's browser. This is clearly different from just listing an address or a phone number and may increase the Web publisher's liability. For example, what if the second side contains defamatory material? Are the Web sites linking to that site and delivering pages to their users also responsible for disseminating that defamatory content? Is there a moral or legal duty to review a site before establishing a link?

None of these issues have been properly sorted out, and few legal precedents are available to offer guidance. The legal nuances of all this will undoubtedly be determined by seminal lawsuits that will resolve some of these matters. But how might we assess linking from a strictly moral point of view? This is a complex and multifaceted question, so we will confine our analysis to two issues: (1) is there an absolute right to link to other Web sites in cyberspace with impunity? and (2) is the Web site publisher who links to another site morally accountable in any way for the content of that second site?

Beyond any doubt, linking is a valuable social good that is consistent with the chief purpose of the Internet: open communication and the seamless availability of information. Hence, in most cases, linking should be encouraged, and it should not be necessary to seek permission every time a link is made to another Web site. Rather, it seems reasonable to assume that participation in the World Wide Web implies permission to link. However, it does not imply an unrestricted right to link to any site *in any manner*. The relevant moral principle here seems to be *autonomy*, the right to exercise control over one's property. If autonomy is duly respected, Web site publishers initiating hyperlinks will refrain from imposing their activities on target Web sites to accept those links. Most Web sites will welcome incoming links, but if a Web site makes it clear that it does not want any incoming links or desires to license those links, this preference should be honored. In addition, a target Web site should also be able to dictate the specific terms of how those links will be constructed. Thus, in the Microsoft-Ticketmaster dispute, Ticketmaster should probably have allowed the link but Microsoft should have respected Ticketmaster's preference to have the link be made to the home page instead of to a subsidiary page. These simple constraints on linking will demonstrate proper respect for the autonomy of Web site producers. At the same time, Web sites should not arbitrarily restrict linking because this dilutes the social value of open communication.

This brings us to the more difficult question of liability—should we hold Web site publishers accountable for any defamatory or damaging material at the linked Web site? On one hand, the Web site publisher is delivering the content of the second page to the user's browser and therefore is directly contributing to the dissemination of the defamatory material. Yet it does seem burdensome to expect a Web site publisher to be intimately familiar with the material on the secondary Web sites to which it links. There must be some level of responsibility here, but it is difficult to fix precisely what that level should be. For example, if a publisher sets up a civics class Web site for a high school and inadvertently links to a Web site with pornography (for instance, www.whitehouse.com instead of www.whitehouse.gov) there is an unmistakable responsibility for misdirecting these students. In general, a Web site publisher should have at a minimum a general familiarity with the contents of the sites to which he or she is linking. It is not too burdensome to expect a cursory overview of the site, but it does seem extreme to require intimate knowledge of all the subsidiary pages. The moral principle "ought implies can" is apposite here.

Thus, in summary, responsible and prudent linking policies would encompass the following: avoid linking to sites that explicitly prohibit such linking; link in the manner requested by the site to which one is linking; have a general familiarity with the content of the linked site to avoid misdirecting one's users; and finally, avoid any impression or indication that the linkage implies an endorsement in any way of one's own products or services.

Ticketmaster and Microsoft settled their lawsuit out of court in early 1999, and both parties agreed not to disclose the terms of the settlement.

However, Microsoft did agree to point visitors to the Ticketmaster home page instead of a page deep within the Ticketmaster site. The legal community hoped that this case would establish a precedent on linking, but so far, that has not happened. As a consequence, there is still some ambiguity about the legal propriety of deep linking.

Another practice related to linking is called *framing*. This occurs when the Web page publisher includes within his or her Web page material from another Web page in a frame or block on the screen. For example, one might link to another site and display some content from that site within a frame of the initial Web page with the advertising or promotional material of the second site concealed. A lawsuit filed by the *Journal Gazette* in Fort Wayne, Indiana, against the Ft-Wayne.com Web site alleges that the site's framing techniques are equivalent to theft of its material. The Web site linked to articles in the paper and by using framing "altered the display of the newspaper's article by placing its own ads and site address in the browser window."[19]

According to Esther Dyson, this sort of framing "harms the content provider trying to sell advertising or simply wanting to maintain its own identity."[20] Those who are the "victims" of framing, such as the *Journal Gazette,* often allege unfair competition and looting of their intellectual property, whereas those who initiate the framing contend that they are merely providing a convenient one-stop-shopping service to their users. They are developing new forms of Web content, which clearly furthers the public interest. Framing is a complex question, and like many other matters on the Internet, this practice requires more scrutiny by moralists and legal specialists.

## ▶ Meta Tags

Meta tags are invisible codes that are incorporated into HTML, that is, the hypertext markup language that is used to construct Web sites. Their name is derived from the practice of "tagging" all of the objects on a Web page—for example, the title of the page is included within title tags. Meta tags represent a brief description or summary of a Web page's contents, usually no longer than one or two words. The Web page for the Museum of Fine Arts (MFA) in Boston might include the following meta tags to describe its Web page: MFA, art museum, Boston, Museum of Fine Arts, etc. Although these codes cannot be seen by the user, they will be recognized by search engines looking for specific sites. If someone enters the search term *MFA* into a search engine, one of the Web sites retrieved will be the site for the Museum of Fine Arts.

Because meta tags are virtually nontransparent, their use is difficult to monitor. How can we be sure that a Web site has "tagged" its contents accurately and honestly? According to Meek Jun, "meta tags often contain popular search terms that have little or nothing to do with the content of the relevant HTML page but are nevertheless inserted for purposes of luring Internet users to a particular Web site."[21]

The legal battle being waged between Terri Welles and Playboy Enterprises Inc. epitomizes the stakes involved in the use of meta tags. Ms. Welles was a Playboy bunny and a centerfold model in 1981; she now operates a Web site that features photos of herself and other models, biographical material, and a personal appearance calendar. The site's meta tags include the words *Playmate* and *Playboy*. Playboy Enterprises has objected to this, contending that the Playmate or Playboy meta tag implies an ongoing affiliation with the "Playboy empire." Welles' use of this tag, they argue, will confuse users who will be misdirected to her site instead of those directly connected to Playboy Enterprises.

When Ms. Welles refused to desist from using the tag, the company filed a $5 million trademark infringement suit, but the initial judgment has not gone in its favor. The ruling stipulated that Welles "could use the trademarked terms in her meta tag because they accurately reflected the contents of her site."[22] In November 1998, the company lost its first appeal, but it has vowed to keep fighting.

Unless it is overturned, the Playboy case may establish a firm legal precedent, but it seems likely that a more nuanced legal solution will be essential if meta tags are not to be abused. Simply because a trademarked name reflects the contents of a Web page, does that mean that it can then be used as a tag? If I write extensively about the Boston Celtics on my amateur sports news Web page does that mean that I should be allowed to embed the phrase *Boston Celtics* in the site's meta tags? This is a legitimate interpretation of Judge Keep's ruling, but users would be ill-served by granting such wide latitude in the use of terms as meta tags. On the other hand, in this test case, Welles has done more than merely write about Playmates. She has had a direct and prolonged affiliation with this organization, which does give her Web site a certain credibility. Therefore, one could argue that this makes her right to the use of these terms more compelling.

As we have intimated, a serious moral problem that often emerges in the use of meta tags is deception. When meta tags are clearly being used only to deceive and mislead users, the moral case against them seems evident. Tags should not be casually used to fool search engines and lure unsuspecting users from the sites they were seeking. For example, if an on-line toy seller embeds the word *disney.store* in its HTML to lure away those looking for the real Disney store Web site, the toy seller is engaging in a crude deception about its association with Disney in order to attract customers under false pretenses. This amounts to false advertising.

There are, however, tough cases like the one involving Ms. Welles and Playboy Enterprises. This is not a straightforward case of deception. The keywords like *Playboy* are not being used to create a false belief of connection because there was some connection in the past that lends credibility to Welles' current activities. Although Welles may end up being on dubious legal ground, it is far from certain that her actions violate any basic moral principles.

## ▶ Creative Integrity

The final issue under consideration is termed *creative integrity* because it involves the ability of authors to maintain control over their artistic and literary works on the Internet. Technology enables viewers of these works to become authors themselves—to transform and recreate digital images that they encounter on the Internet and to retransmit those images throughout cyberspace.

Do such activities violate trademark and copyright laws? Do they infringe on a creator's well-earned property rights? Should authors have the prerogative to prevent the parody and manipulation of their materials on the Internet?

An infamous case that has brought these issues to the fore is the "Distorted Barbie." This represents a Web art reproduction of Barbie that has been digitally modified as a commentary on the Barbie doll icon of American culture. The artist who created this is Mark Napier, and on a Web site sponsored by his supporters, one can find the following description of his creation:

> Artist Mark Napier is the author and creator of The Distorted Barbie, a Web-based exploration in words and images of the impact Barbie and all her baggage have had on our bodies and culture. The site is a poetic and potent piece of Internet art.[23]

Barbie's "owner," the Mattel toy company, was not swayed by any of this. It strongly protested and demanded that this distorted Barbie be immediately removed from Napier's Web site (Interport). Mattel and its lawyers have invoked the "moral rights" defense. Moral rights, a translation of the French term *droit moral,* bestows on an author control over the fate of his or her works. In the United States, moral rights are protected by the law embodied in the Visual Artists Rights Act of 1990 (VARA), which applies only to the visual arts. According to VARA, a creator has the right to prevent revision, modification, or distortion of his or her work. The visual arts protected by VARA include paintings, drawings, prints, sculptures, and photographs taken to be shown at an exhibition. VARA protects works only of "recognized stature."

VARA gives an author two basic rights: (1) the right of attribution and (2) the right of integrity. The first right protects an author's work from being attributed to someone else. The right of integrity bars distortion or alteration that might impair the author's reputation or stature as an artist. Should VARA apply to the distorted Barbie or to parodies of other commercial products?

Here again, we encounter the familiar conflict between property rights and free speech, which has been a common theme in this entire chapter. Napier's site is not seeking commercial gains from Barbie, and it would appear that his creation is a form of art. Hence, at present, it seems to be a legitimate form of fair use, similar in some ways to Andy Warhol's reproductions of Brillo boxes and Campbell's soup cans. Like Warhol, Napier is simply using popular commercial products as the raw material and inspiration for his artistic endeavors. It seems perfectly logical in this age "where girls bond with Barbie and dream of broadcast exploits of Sabrina the teenage witch," that this would become the stuff of creative activity.[24] In certain key respects, the distorted Barbie, however offensive some may find it, offers a valuable commentary on this era not for commercial gains but for its own sake. Such artistic impulses should not be stifled by excessively broad copyright and trademark restrictions.

We admit that the Distorted Barbie is one of many tough cases that make it so difficult to sustain that precarious but necessary balance between fair use and intellectual property protection. However, suppression of artistic reproductions based on commercial icons seems to err on the side of overprotecting the Internet.

## Discussion Questions

1. What limits, if any, should there be on a user's right to link to other Web sites? Should there be laws clarifying and protecting the right to link?
2. What is the significance of the open code movement? Comment on the pros and cons of open code software.
3. Explain how trademark ownership can conflict with free speech rights. How should these competing claims be resolved?
4. Comment on this observation from Esther Dyson's essay titled "Intellectual Property on the 'net": "The issue isn't that intellectual property laws should (or will) disappear; rather, they will simply become less important in the scheme of things."[25]

## CASE STUDY

### The www.nga Domain Name Dispute (Hypothetical)

The National Gun Association (NGA) of America is a powerful lobbying organization established more than fifty years ago to protect the public's constitutional right to own firearms. The organization has millions of members concentrated in the western and southern regions of the country. It has a strong presence in Washington, D.C., where it advocates against efforts to restrict the right to own a gun. The NGA's vocal support of that right has spawned opposition groups, which believe that the NGA helps contribute to a climate of violence through its encouragement of gun ownership.

The NGA has a Web site, www.nga.org, where it disseminates information about the right to bear arms and other issues related to gun ownership and gun control. The site also informs members about impending legislation and advises them how to register their opinions with elected officials. The Web site is popular with members and averages more than 25,000 hits a day.

One of the more radical groups opposing the NGA, called Pacifists for Gun Control (PGC), has set up a nonprofit organization that distributes literature and organizes its own lobbying efforts. It has created a Web site for which it was able to secure the domain name www.nga-assassins.org. The PGC has admitted that one purpose in using this accusatory domain name is to intercept users looking for www.nga.org through its meta tags. Its home page has the following message:

**Don't be fooled by the NGA.**
**Look here to see the damage that guns can really do!**

The PGC's Web site is filled with material on the perils of gun ownership and the virtues of gun controls, particularly for automatic weapons and handguns. There are also links to other sites that discuss the excesses and the tendentious views of the NGA. Through the contents of this Web page, the PGC seeks to convert gun owners and others sympathetic to the NGA's objectives to its ideological views regarding violence and firearms.

The NGA has filed a lawsuit to block this Web site on the grounds that the domain name is deceptive and misleading. It also alleges that its trademark, "NGA," has been violated and diluted. The PGC contends that it is merely exercising its free speech rights. It is using this derivative domain name to help propagate its political ideas about gun ownership. It also points out that NGA members who are temporarily diverted to this site can easily move on to the real NGA Web site, so no harm is done. A court in the NGA's home state of Texas has taken up the matter and will soon issue a preliminary ruling.

## Questions

1. Is this a free speech issue? Does the PGC have any right to use the domain name www.nga-assassins.org?
2. If you were litigating this case on behalf of the National Gun Association, which arguments would you use to support their position?
3. Can the PGC's unorthodox actions be morally justified in any way?

## CASE STUDY

### Framing as Property Theft?

In May 1998, a significant property dispute arose between *The Journal Gazette*, a major daily newspaper published in Fort Wayne, Indiana, and a Web site called www.Ft-Wayne.com. This Web site was created as a public service to provide announcements about community activities and local social events in Fort Wayne and its environs.

The newspaper alleged that when the Web site linked to its newspaper articles, the article would appear within a "frame," that is, surrounded by Ft-Wayne.com's own ads and banners along with its site address. *The Journal Gazette* filed suit against the Web site, claiming that its property was being systematically "looted'" by this practice. The lawsuit cited federal trademark and copyright infringement as the basis for its claim. *The Journal Gazette* also alleged that Ft.Wayne.com was acting as a free rider by exhibiting the *Journal's* articles surrounded by its own advertisements.

The Ft-Wayne.com Web site did stop framing the newspaper's articles after the lawsuit was filed but insisted that it did not violate any laws or do anything wrong. Defenders of the Web site observed that they were guilty only of providing more readers for *The Journal Gazette*. One of the Web site's creators also defended the practice "as a means to keep viewers from roaming away form the Ft-Wayne. com site."[26]

### Questions

1. Comment on the merits of this lawsuit. Should there be unambiguous laws that prohibit framing? Does it make any difference that this was a community service site?
2. Defenders of framing use the analogy that this practice is similar to a newsstand running advertising banners over the area where it sells its newspapers. Does this analogy make any sense to you?

### References

1. Samuelson, P. 1997. Confab clips copyright cartel. *Wired* 5.03:62.
2. Honore. 1961. Ownership. In Guest, A. G. (Ed.). *Oxford essays in jurisprudence.* Oxford: Oxford University Press, p. 108.
3. DeLong, J. V. 1997. *Property matters.* New York: The Free Press, p. 340.
4. Background material in this section was found in Liu, J. Overview of trademark law. Available at Harvard Law School Web site, http://cyber.harvard.edu/law.
5. Bender, D. 1982.*Computer law: Evidence and procedure.* New York: M. Bender, p. 4A-2.
6. Hanneman, H. 1985. *The patentability of computer software.* Deventer, The Netherlands: Kluwer Academic Publishers, p. 87.

7. Hughes, J. 1997. Philosophy of intellectual property. In Moore, A. (Ed.). *Intellectual property*. Lanham, MD: Rowman & Littlefield, p. 121.
8. Reeve, A. 1986. *Property*. Atlantic Highlands, NJ: Humanities Press, p. 137.
9. Boyle, J. 1996. *Shamans, software and spleens: Law and the construction of the information society*. Cambridge, MA: Harvard University Press, p. 23.
10. For more about Boyle's important book, see my review of *Shamans, software and spleens*, which appears in *Ethics and information technology* 1(2):161–163, 1999. Some of the material here is drawn from that review.
11. Stefik, M. 1997. Trusted systems. *Scientific American*, March, p. 79.
12. Stallman, R. 1985. GNU manifesto. Available at www.gnu.org/manifesto.html.
13. Raymond, E. The cathedral and the bazaar. Available at http://www.tuxedo.org/~esr/writings/cathedral-bazaar.
14. Leonard, A. 1999. Open season. *Wired*, May, p. 142.
15. Samuelson, P., et al. 1996. A new view of intellectual property and software. *Communications of the ACM* 39(3):24.
16. Macavinta, C. 1998. Scientologists in trademark dispute. *CNET News.com*, January 29.
17. Madoff, E. 1997. Freedom to link under attack. *New York Law Journal*, June 23.
18. Ibid.
19. Kaplan, C. Lawsuit may determine whether framing is thieving. *Cyber Law Journal*. Available at http://www.nytimes.com/library/tech/98/05/cyberlaw.
20. Dyson, E. 1998. *Release 2.1*. New York: Random House, p. 199.
21. Jun, M. 1997. Meta tags: The case of the invisible infringer. *The New York Law Journal*, October 24.
22. Kaplan, C. 1998. Former Playmate wins round in fight over Web site labels. *Cyber Law Journal*, November 13. Available at http://www.nytimes.com/library/tech/98/11/cyberlaw.
23. See Napier's Web site, http://ezone.org/ez/e7/articles/napier/barbie.html.
24. Mann, C. 1998. Who will own your next great idea. *Atlantic Monthly*, September, p. 183.
25. Dyson, E. 1994. Intellectual property on the net. In *Release 1.0*. New York: Random House.
26. Kaplan, C. Lawsuit.

# CHAPTER FIVE

# Regulating Internet Privacy

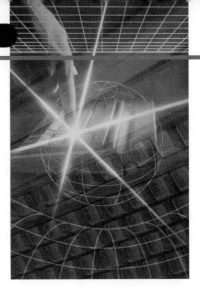

## ▶ Introduction

The Information Age has created an open society where privacy seems to grow scarcer with each technological innovation. The Internet and its supporting architectures have made it much easier to track and monitor individual behavior. Personal information in the Internet economy has become even more of a commodity that can be sold, exchanged, or recombined with relative ease. Identifying serial numbers embedded within computers or software programs that allow traces to the end user threaten to end the electronic anonymity that has so far characterized many interactions in cyberspace.

The public seems to be ambivalent and even nonchalant about privacy issues until their collective consciousness is jarred by some startling new revelation. On occasion, some organization discovers that it has transgressed a certain threshold, and it is forced to placate disgruntled customers. For example, in July 1997, America Online (AOL) was sharply rebuked when it announced a plan to provide lists of its customers' telephone numbers to selected telemarketers. AOL had a long-standing practice of selling lists of its subscribers names and addresses, but those lists did not include e-mail addresses or phone numbers. Its customers feared that they would receive intrusive phone solicitations and that this piece of data might be a link to other personal information.

In addition, as a result of sophisticated surveillance and monitoring technologies, the networked workplace has become a virtual panopticon where workers' movements and interactions are more visible than ever before to their managers. Hence, the employee's right to privacy, which was once gaining some respect in this venue, now appears to be in real peril.

Privacy is threatened in many other environments as well, and its co-existence with the Internet and electronic commerce (e-commerce) seems to be particularly tenuous. The debate over privacy continues to intensify, and there is little doubt that this issue will be a dominant ethical concern for many years to come. As Marc Rotenberg has observed, "Privacy will be to the information economy of the next century what consumer protection and environmental concerns have been to the industrial society of the 20th century."[1]

What are the ramifications of this steady erosion of personal and work-place privacy? Once lost, can it ever be retrieved? What are reasonable expectations for some sort of privacy protection as one retrieves information from the Internet or shops at Web sites hungry for consumer data? Are children at an even greater risk for invasions of privacy by benign-looking Web sites? What is the appropriate scope of privacy protection in the workplace? Finally, do some privacy protections go too far and undermine free speech rights in cyberspace?

We will attempt to consider these and other related questions in this chapter, but first we must review why the right to privacy is of fundamental importance from a legal as well as from a moral perspective. This will help us appreciate why its gradual but persistent erosion cannot be taken so lightly.

## ▶ A Definition and Theory of Privacy

Privacy is not a simple concept that can be defined easily. Perhaps the most basic and inclusive definition dates back to a seminal *Harvard Law Review* article written by Samuel Warren and Louis Brandeis in 1890. They differentiated the right to privacy from other legal rights and defined it as the right to be left alone, that is, the right to some measure of solitude in one's life.

This general definition is a good starting point, but it is obviously inadequate because the "right to be left alone" is rather broad and imprecise. A more suitable definition has been formulated by Ruth Gavison. She defines privacy as the limitation of others' access to an individual with three key elements: secrecy, anonymity, and solitude. Anonymity refers to the protection from undesired attention, solitude is the lack of physical proximity to others, and secrecy (or confidentiality) involves limiting the dissemination of knowledge about oneself.[2] Although the right to anonymity, secrecy, and solitude must be subject to certain limits for anyone who participates in civil society, Gavison has laid the groundwork for a nuanced understanding of the right to privacy.

It is also possible to distinguish several types of privacy, such as psychological privacy or communication privacy. The focus of our attention, however, is primarily *information privacy.* It concerns the collection, use, and dissemination of information about individuals. The right to informational privacy is the right to control the disclosure of and access to one's personal information.

Philosophers have made many attempts to ground or justify this right to privacy, but the most convincing approach regards the right to privacy as an instrumental value, which supports other basic rights such as property, bodily security, and freedom. A primary moral foundation for the value of privacy is its role as a condition of freedom (or autonomy): a shield of privacy is absolutely essential if one is to freely pursue his or her projects or cultivate intimate social relationships.

According to James Reiman, without privacy there are two ways in which our freedom can be appreciably attenuated.[3] First, there is the risk of an *extrinsic loss of freedom* because the lack of privacy often makes individuals vulnerable to having their behavior controlled by others. Sensitive information collected without one's permission and knowledge can be a potent weapon in the hands of those in positions of authority. Such information might be used to deprive individuals of certain rewards and opportunities, such as job promotions or transfers, or may preclude eligibility for insurance and other important necessities. This thwarts our autonomy, our basic capacity for making choices and directing our lives without outside interference. As Carol Gould has observed, "privacy is a protection against unwanted imposition or coercion by others and thus a protection of one's freedom of action."[4]

There is also the risk of *an intrinsic loss of freedom.* It is common knowledge that most people will behave differently when they are being watched or monitored by others. In these circumstances, it is normal to feel more inhibited and tentative about one's plans and activities. As Richard Wassestrom puts it, without privacy life is often "less spontaneous and more measured."[5]

In summary, without the benefit of privacy, we are more subject to the manipulation and control by others and we are more inhibited and timid about the pursuit of our goals and activities. Foucault believes that this is precisely the "panoptic effect" that most prison systems seek to achieve whereby the inmate feels that he or she is in a "state of conscious and permanent visibility that assures the automatic functioning of power."[6] But do we really want to establish such demoralizing conditions in our homes and offices?

James Moor has developed a similar justification of privacy. Recall his contention that there are shared "core values" that are basic for human existence. These values include life, happiness, freedom, knowledge, ability, resources, and security. Although privacy is not a core value, according to Moor, it is the expression of a core value, that is, the value of security. Without privacy, it is difficult to be and feel secure. Moreover, privacy takes on special significance in a computerized networked culture, which poses strong risks for privacy and hence for our personal security. According to Moor, "people have a basic right to be protected, which from the point of view of our computerized culture, includes privacy protection."[7] Therefore, privacy is in effect elevated to the same level as the other core values because in our information intensive culture some degree of privacy is essential for security and by extension for human flourishing.

On the surface, almost everyone recognizes the validity of these arguments and the significance of the right to privacy. We all want some measure of privacy and solitude in our lives. Problems arise because the right to privacy often conflicts with other basic rights, and the task of determining which right should take priority is a formidable challenge for ethicists and public policy makers. The most serious conflict is between privacy and free speech. For example, some free speech advocates regard privacy regulations as a form of censorship because they conflict with an organization's right to communicate or transmit information. If we protect privacy through more comprehensive laws, they argue, we risk losing the right to freely exchange valuable consumer data.

As we shall see, the threats to one's autonomy and personal security are heightened by using the Internet because one's zone of privacy is appreciably diminished in this open and fluid environment. We first consider the precise nature of those threats and then discuss some appropriate policy responses.

## ▶ Personal Information on the Internet

Novice Internet users are often astonished to learn about the plethora of personal data that is now available on-line. Consider the following scenario. Suppose that you live in a leafy suburb of Milwaukee and that you are curious about your new eccentric neighbor. Something about her demeanor is rather unsettling and unusual. So you decide to do some investigating, even though you don't even know her name. You know only her address, but that is sufficient to get started: the Infospace search engine's "Find neighbor's" option quickly allows you to find other information about your neighbor, such as her name and phone number using the reverse lookup option, which requires only an address to initiate the search. You then access another popular search engine, AltaVista, and this search turns up the name of the company she works for. You then go to the Milwaukee City Tax Assessment Online database, key in the address, and within seconds, you know the assessed value of her property, her current property tax, and the fact that she has a partial personal exemption because she is a surviving spouse.

You have spent about 15 minutes on the Internet, and you have just begun scratching the surface of this woman's background. You could continue and probably build a pretty thorough profile of this woman by using other search engines and Web sites. But where does one draw the line in the search for another individual's personal data? Has anything immoral happened here in this incident of "cybersnooping"? Does it make any difference if we make no revelations to others or take no actions based on our findings? Is there anything wrong with the search engines that facilitate this process? Should this type of data be subject to regulation to limit on-line stalking and similar abuses? Should on-line privacy be a priority for public policy makers?

The question we must first consider is whether information residing on the Internet should be so "public" and hence easily accessible. Most of the data that has become fodder for search engines existed in a public or pseudopublic format (such as a phone book and court records) and has now become digitized. On one level, it is difficult to see anything wrong with this. Converting information into an electronic format and providing a better mechanism to search that data seems to be perfectly acceptable. Civil libertarians have long argued for the freedom of information in a democratic society because the alternative leads to secrecy and governmental control of information.

On the other hand, personal data are being made available in these on-line databases, which are accessible to search engines without our knowledge and consent. Furthermore, there is more going on here than a mere conversion of data from hard copy to digital format. The Internet makes the data globally and instantaneously accessible. As the curious neighbor, you probably would not pore through documents stored in City Hall for hours to find out about your neighbor, but if it just takes 15 minutes on the Internet, the temptation to snoop is greater. Also, what makes this data more of a threat is the possibility for recombination of disparate and hitherto unconnected data elements. Our hypothetical example illustrated that with little effort, a fairly thorough profile of someone could be constructed. This could create some potential for mischief, and as a result, many people will soon prefer to keep their backgrounds as concealed as possible.

Thus, there is a *qualitative* difference between the requirements to physically track down data and the ease of finding it on the Internet with the aid of search engines. But is the answer stricter government regulation of on-line databases? The problem is that such regulations could have an unwanted chilling effect on the distribution and accessibility of valid information.

A feasible alternative might be to work out a responsible middle ground between an outright ban (or detailed restrictions) and a completely laissez-faire approach. Certain data elements should *never* be in a public, on-line database, and this includes Social Security numbers, which are a link to a wealth of other sensitive information. These databases should also exclude mothers' maiden name information, which is used for identification verification at banks and other financial institutions. The ethical justification is that the potential for harm increases exponentially when such items are made so readily available.

So far, this is a line that on-line databases have not yet crossed, but they have tested the waters. In 1996, LEXIS-NEXIS, a company that collects personal data on millions of people and resells it to subscribers, provoked the ire of regulators and privacy advocates when it began including Social Security numbers, birth dates, and mothers' maiden names on its "P-Trak" database. The company did reverse itself and has vowed to exclude these items from its reference lists.

If we try to harmonize the need for freedom of information and the imperative of privacy, it is reasonable to conclude that on-line data systems are not inherently immoral or a social nuisance. However, we propose that there should be some limits and conditions, such as the following:

- Exclusion of sensitive unique identifiers such as Social Security numbers, birth dates, and mothers' maiden names

- Exclusion of all unlisted phone numbers

- Clear provision of an opt-out option so that people can have their names promptly removed from a database

- Prohibition of reverse Social Security number look-ups

## ▶ Consumer Privacy on the Internet

Prior to the Information Age, the transactions that occurred between vendors and consumers were private affairs, nobody's business but the two parties involved. They were also quickly forgotten. The local baker knew you by name but probably couldn't remember what sort of breads and pastries you purchased last month. This has changed rather dramatically in the information economy because computers can remember everything for an indefinite time. If we use a shopping card at our local supermarket, a data warehouse is storing the details of our purchases, and sometimes this data is shared with food producers and others for targeted marketing campaigns.

There are two distinct phases to this systematic loss of our privacy as consumers. The first might aptly be labeled as the "database phase." The emergence of database technology in the early 1980s made it possible to store, retrieve, and disseminate copious amounts of information efficiently and economically. During this period, our personal data were transferred to computerized records, which became the foundation of consumer profiles. These profiles were often based on public records sold by government agencies at the state and local levels. For example, car registration and license information has been digitized and relied on as a major source of marketing data to reach certain groups of consumers.

Another source of data for these systems is the information generated by various consumer transactions, such as telephone or mail orders, memberships, warranty cards, or even rebate coupons. This information too can serve as the building blocks for richly detailed customer records. Pharmaceutical companies, for example, build their databases from consumers who call 800 numbers, subscribe to magazines, or fill out pharmacy questionnaires.

The popular retailer Consumer Value Stores (CVS) recently sent a mailing to diabetic patients advertising a new breakthrough drug Rezulin. CVS contracted with a direct mail marketing firm to mine its prescription databases for insulin users. Everyone on this customer list was then sent the literature from CVS, although the mailing was funded by Warner-Lambert, which makes Rezulin. Some consumers were incensed by this violation of their right to patient confidentiality and resented that CVS singled them out as diabetic patients. Despite this backlash, the company has defended the mailings because they provided valuable information for their customers.[8]

Some corporations, such as Metromail, function exclusively as data brokers. They specialize in aggregating and maintaining myriad data about consumers. Metromail's National Consumer Data Base includes detailed information on 103 million people in the United States. Metromail is especially proficient in tracking important transitions in people's lives. For example, if someone has moved to a new house, their name will be provided to junk mailers or other vendors for 25 cents a name. These individuals are obviously prospects for new home furnishings and appliances, long distance telephone service, and so forth.

The use of data warehouse software and more sophisticated storage devices such as optical disk technology has greatly aided the preservation of voluminous consumer data. It has also made possible data mining activities. American Airlines' Sabre Group was recently pilloried in the press when it announced plans to build a data warehouse of its travel reservation information, which would then be made available for sale to outside agencies.[9]

Thanks to the Internet, if Sabre were to sell that data, it could be transferred effortlessly over this global network. This easy transmission of stored data and the heavy reliance on the Internet and on private digital networks to help conduct business has ushered in the "network phase." Consumers routinely communicate with vendors by e-mail, post messages to electronic bulletin boards on the Internet, and visit Web sites where they can browse an on-line catalog and purchase products. In this phase, information has become more mobile than ever before, and connectivity facilitates an unprecedented level of monitoring of personal behavior.

The steady ascendance of e-commerce has meant that the new battleground for consumer privacy protection is now shifting to Web site vendors. A 1998 survey by the Federal Trade Commission (FTC) found that 92% of commercial Web sites collect personal information, but only 14% disclose their information gathering practices to consumers.[10] Some of these sites are selling this information, often without the users' knowledge or consent.

Sometimes, users are promised certain goods in exchange for personal background information. For example, Catilina Marketing Corporation provides consumers with on-line supermarket coupons in exchange for their personal shopping card number and demographic information. This information is then resold to its coupon and marketing clients.

This sudden surge of Web-based activity has led to some particularly egregious violations of privacy. Consider the problematic case of Geocities, an on-line community of 2 million personal Web sites. In late summer 1998, it was forced to revise its information collection policies to avoid an FTC lawsuit. New members of Geocities seeking to establish their own personal Web sites were required to fill out a registration form and had to supply information such as their exact income along with their level of education. Members were assured that Geocities "would not share this information without their permission, but will use it to gain a better understanding of who is visiting Geocities."[11] According to the FTC, however, such "permission" was granted as long as the user did not check a box that would allow one to opt out of future marketing offers. Most users in fact did not check this box, and as a result, their information was widely distributed to other Internet companies such as CMG Information Services or Infobeat. At a minimum, Geocities is culpable of deceiving its customers. It should have abided by its promise not to distribute personal information as sensitive as salary data, and it should have provided a lucid and straightforward mechanism so that users could grant their permission to have that data disclosed.

There are particularly strong concerns about on-line marketing to children who are beginning to visit commercial Web sites in greater numbers. Some advertisers use their Web sites to collect personal information from children. This information perhaps becomes the basis for targeted e-mail messages sent by a favorite cartoon character. Another 1998 FTC survey determined that 89% of 212 child-oriented Web sites collected personal information from children and only half of those sites disclosed their information collection practices.[12] According to the FTC, all sites engaging in this practice should disclose their practices and provide some form of parental control over the collection of this personal data.

As we have suggested, the legal system in the United States has lagged behind the steady erosion of privacy that has resulted from some of these practices. Part of the reason for this can be attributed to the political power of data brokers and other corporations who make their money by manipulating information. There is also a recognition that information sharing and a concomitant loss of privacy are inevitable in an information economy. Targeted information is the key to marketing success in an economy where so many product variations and consumer choices exist.

Even if we concede this point, it does not mean that current practices or a laissez-faire attitude is completely acceptable. Reasonable standards must be established to minimize harm to consumers—companies must take seriously their stewardship responsibilities, provide at least a reasonable way to opt-out of these lists and mailings, and develop some mechanism for parental consent for the collection of data from minors.

Finally, we must consider the "cookie problem." One way in which Web site vendors can track the movement of their customers is the use of cookies. These "cookies" are small data files that are written and stored on the user's hard disk drive by a Web site when the user visits that site with a browser. They contain information such as passwords, lists of pages within the Web site that have been visited, and the dates when those pages were last examined. When the user revisits the Web site that stored the cookie, the user's computer system quietly sends the cookie back with all of its relevant information.

Cookies represent a modest means of monitoring users' movements when they visit a particular Web site. If a customer visits an on-line bookstore, a cookie can reveal whether he or she browses through sports books or is more apt to look at books on wine and gourmet foods. If a user comes to this store merely to window shop in cyberspace, cookies can provide the retailer with valuable information that could be the basis of a targeted promotion for their next visit.

Although most Web merchants see cookies in benign terms, there is some reason to be concerned about this technology because it does function as a form of covert surveillance that conjures up an unsettling "Big Brother" image. After all, cookie technology is analogous to having someone follow you through the mall with a video camera. Are cookies just a nuisance or can they cause real damage?

There is certainly some potential for harm in the way cookies are currently handled. What if off-beat or pornographic Web sites visited on a whim send their respective visitors cookies without their knowledge? Those cookies are residing on one's hard drive and could be opened by a nosy employer or someone else with access to that computer. Also, Web sites could begin to package and resell this data that they have acquired by watching their customers. Amazon.com has collected an enormous amount of information about the reading habits of its customers and, according to sources at the company, has not "ruled out" selling this to interested third parties.

From a moral perspective, the primary issue appears to be the consumer's loss of autonomy. Should any company be allowed to deposit a cookie file on a user's hard drive without the user's knowledge and consent? One could argue that this is presumptuous and disrespectful of a user's right to control his or her "private space," which should include the disk space of his or her personal computers. When things are delivered to our physical space without our consent (for example, junk mail), we at least know about them. What is so troublesome about cookies is that most users have no idea that these files tracking their movements have been accepted by their computer systems.

There is actually a fairly simple solution to this problem. A policy of informed consent might go a long way to making cookie technology morally palatable for those who have a problem with this technology. Browsers already have the capability to prompt users before they accept a cookie, but the default setting is to let Web sites transmit these files without asking that question. Instead, the default setting could be altered so that users are always given this option before any transmission is made.

Many commercial Web sites that use cookies, however, maintain that they really do no harm, and they conclude that such corrective action is unnecessary. At worst, they are an annoyance, easily handled by users who can set their Web browsers not to place cookies on their computer systems.

## ▶ Medical Privacy

Another imminent threat to privacy has developed in the health care industry, where patients records are being put on-line to reduce costs and increase convenience for customers. Insurers, health maintenance organizations (HMOs), and doctors are beginning to use the Internet to provide patients with personal medical information, such as test results or payment records. Soon the HMO Kaiser Permanente will begin providing laboratory results to its patients over the Internet. Each patient will be given a personal identification number (PIN) to obtain his or her records. Doctors are also beginning to communicate with their patients through e-mail. Their patients like this accessibility and convenience but voice concerns about security and privacy. Furthermore, the impetus for on-line medical data was given a boost by a doctor in Appalachia, who with the consent of his patients, has placed their medical records on the World Wide Web. The hope is that if one of his patients must visit an emergency room in this rural area, the medical staff there can quickly learn about the patient's medical history by logging on to the Internet.

The main privacy concern is that a growing number of third-party companies handling medical information will be given access to the sensitive and revealing patient data that is going on-line.

Consider what already happens with pharmaceutical data. Several companies, such as IMS America and PCN (Physicians Computer Network), specialize in gathering information on patient illnesses and the drugs that have been prescribed for those illnesses. They are given direct access to the databases maintained by hospitals, HMOs, and pharmacies to generate this information, which is highly sought after by the pharmaceutical industry. The patient's name and other personal data is supposed to be stripped away when these records are captured. But IMS has admitted that patient names are often included when they purchase this data from HMOs or drug store chains. This company is careful enough to remove those names along with other identifiers, but will other companies that get into this business be as conscientious?

Obviously, the practice itself raises many questions. Is it morally acceptable for physicians and pharmacists to entrust such sensitive information to these brokers without the knowledge and consent of their patients? Is such a practice truly consistent with the obligations of information stewardship? And shouldn't there be stricter safeguards to ensure that personal identifiers (name, Social Security number) are *never* included with this data?

When laboratory results become available on-line, who else besides the doctor and patient will be authorized to see them? Will certain third parties be given access? If the wide availability of prescription drug data sets any precedent, these laboratory results may be far less confidential than people think.

Thus, medical privacy, like consumer privacy, may also be destined to become a victim of our sophisticated information technology systems. By putting so much medical data on-line, sometimes without proper safeguards, the government, the health care industry, and the information industry have possibly set the stage to undermine the foundations of the *confidential* doctor–patient relationship. Beyond question, on-line medical data can lead to more efficient health care, but Internet stakeholders must be fully prepared to sacrifice a measure of privacy for that efficiency.

The extreme sensitivity of health care data seems to demand government intervention to impede this erosion of medical privacy. However, the U.S. federal government's recent behavior make it part of the problem, not the solution. When the Clinton Administration announced that it was thinking of assigning every American a unique medical identification number that would track everyone's medical records from birth to death, strident protests erupted. The Administration backed down, and plans for this identifier have been shelved. Such proposals have understandably made many people skeptical about the government's ability to regulate medical privacy with sensitivity and objectivity.

## ▶ Privacy as Censorship?

If strong privacy protections are implemented either through self-regulation, technology, or federal legislation, the domain of free-flowing information will certainly be circumscribed. This will have a negative economic and social impact that must be weighed carefully before such action is pursued.

Opponents of stronger privacy rights have argued that restrictions on information flow to protect privacy are tantamount to censorship. Solveig Singleton of the Cato Institute has embraced this point of view in an influential article that has been highlighted in mainstream business publications such as *The Wall Street Journal* and *Forbes*.[13]

Singleton argues that free speech rights should not be overridden to create new privacy rights. He maintains that consumer databases do not present a new or unique threat and are no worse than more traditional ways of gathering and disseminating information, such as gossip, which was the basis for information exchange before technology. Gossip exchanged freely through informal networks within small communities could cause much more harm than private sector databases, which are at least more accurate and impersonal than gossip. Consumer databases are simply the formalization of more direct information flows that took place between consumers and merchants in those small towns. They represent a more efficient way of keeping track of customers' special needs, their preferences, their credit record, and so forth. Thus, if we do not regulate this more harmful exchange of personal information in private conversation, "we cannot justify regulation of consumer data bases."[14]

Singleton further argues that the collection of information in commercial contexts is no different than the gathering of information that takes place in more informal and casual ways. Information about a person's buying habits "belongs to the person providing the product as well as the person consuming the product."[15] We may be annoyed when vendors use that information to solicit more business, but such annoyance does not justify stringent regulation.

Thus, Singleton concludes that restrictions on the collection of information such as an "opt-in" requirement are unwarranted and represent a "prior restraint" on free speech (consumers must give their explicit permission before information collected for one purpose can be used for another purpose). His outlook changes dramatically, however, when it comes to government databases, which pose a far more serious threat to privacy and autonomy than commercial databases: "Because the state claims so much more power than private parties—power it then abuses—government databases pose terrible risks."[16] This problem is compounded by the government's reliance on a unique identifier, the Social Security number, which allows links of sensitive data.

Is there any merit to these arguments? Should we be more apprehensive about government or about private corporations? Is data transmission over the Internet just a more streamlined form of good old-fashioned gossip?

Singleton underestimates the dangers attendant upon the misuse of personal information. Sophisticated information technology (IT) systems have the power to capture, recombine, and classify personal information efficiently and inexpensively. A credit card company, for example, may build a record of identifying information (such as name, address, and phone number), include a purchase history, and recombine this with financial data purchased from other sources. These profiles may then be packaged and resold to other interested parties—perhaps insurance companies would like to know more about us before renewing our policies or assessing a premium. As Oscar Gandy has pointed out, this collection and reuse of personal information is part of a broad *panoptic sort,* a "complex discriminatory technology," that is used to sort people into different categories. The danger of the panoptic sort is that "personal information is not only used to *include* individuals with the marketing scan, but may also be used to *exclude* them from other life chances linked to employment, insurance, housing, education, and credit."[17]

IT is much more powerful than local gossip and essentially enables an unprecedented erosion of personal privacy that can have significant and long-lasting consequences. People like local vendors and the town gossips forget most of the minute details they learn about their fellow citizens in day-to-day interactions. But IT systems such as comprehensive data warehouses *never* forget. Also, as people are categorized and profiled, they can become easy targets of discrimination that can eventually exclude them from essential services. They can suffer economic losses and even public embarrassment. These profiles create an asymmetry of information between the consumer and those corporations that provide essential services. This whole process thereby enhances corporate power and diminishes the freedom of consumers.

Thus, the stakes in preserving privacy are much higher than Singleton seems to realize. If it were simply a matter of passing information along electronically instead of through the medium of gossip there would not be such a problem. However, there is much more to the panoptic sort than the mere diffusion of information. Personal data is captured, recombined, and classified so that profiles can be built that categorize people in certain ways. For example, one data broker sells lists of homosexual men by culling periodical subscriptions and even calls to AIDS hotlines. This is only one of many examples of how technology classifies us, initially for the sake of marketing efforts. But as these lists become disseminated throughout cyberspace and combined with other lists, who can predict for what discriminatory purposes they will ultimately be used?

## ▶ Privacy Protection in Europe

For some time, European countries have been developing much stronger privacy protection than countries like the United States, which has tended to rely more heavily on self-regulation. There have been laws on the books throughout Europe that ban telephone marketing along with the selling of personal data for marketing purposes. These laws also generally protect users against "the creation of files from data collected via the Internet; [and] the transfer via the Internet of personal data files."[18]

In addition, European countries such as Germany, the Netherlands, and Sweden have established government agencies dedicated to the objective of privacy protection. In Sweden, the Data Inspection Board (DIB) issues licenses to keepers of commercial databases containing consumer information and carefully monitors any matching or recombining of data from one database system to another.

In the fall of 1998, acting on behalf of all of its member countries, the European Union executed a law prohibiting the buying and selling of personal data. It is known as the EU Directive on Data Protection. According to *The New York Times*, "The goal of the European law is to prohibit companies from using information about their customers in ways the customers never intended—for example, selling it to other companies for use as a marketing tool."[19]

Since the promulgation of this directive, which must be translated into specific laws in the member countries, there have been fears that it would disrupt e-commerce between Europe and the United States. The directive contains a provision that enjoins countries within the European Union from disseminating personal data to any country that does not guarantee the same level of protection. This might mean that Europe could block the transfer of data by multinational corporations that operate in Europe and the United States. This law would also seem to prevent U.S. e-commerce companies from gathering any consumer data from European customers unless it complied with certain privacy standards, even if this activity is typically part of the on-line transaction.

At the heart of the European Directive is the stipulation of basic consumer rights regarding their personal data. These include the right to know when information is collected and how that information will be used, the right to know the identity of those collecting the information, the right to access the information stored in data files, and the right to correct information in those files that is incomplete or inaccurate.

The European approach to privacy protection provides a model for how a systematic regulatory system might function. Aside from a comprehensive legal framework spelling out the privacy rights of consumers, there would be some need for a bureaucratic infrastructure to monitor compliance and to deal with offenders. Although there is no denying the benefits of this model, other governments in both developed and developing countries may be reluctant to invest in that bureaucracy or to assemble an information police force to protect the privacy of their citizens. Yet this may be the only truly efficacious way of offering citizens sustainable privacy protection.

## ▶ Privacy and Internet Architectures

So far in this chapter, we have illustrated some of the key architectures that have contributed to the erosion of privacy. Databases and their retrieval algorithms have permitted the accumulation of vast amounts of personal data that can easily be culled by curious users and opportunistic corporations. On the World Wide Web, architectures like cookie technology make it possible to monitor users as they shop at different Web stores. This architecture could become especially pernicious because it allows data to be collected nontransparently, without the user's cognizance that a cookie has been deposited on the hard drive. What will be the implications for privacy if future Internet architectures continue to work so stealthily?

The debate about Internet architectures and privacy heated up in early 1999 with the introduction of Intel Corporation's plan to put identification numbers in its next generation of computer chips, the Pentium IIIs. The primary purpose of the embedded serial number was to authenticate a user's identity in a business transaction and to allow organizations to better track their computer equipment. Unlike digital certificates, which can be falsified, this appeared to be a much less fallible way of ensuring an individual's true digital identity.

Privacy advocates, however, had a much different perspective, and immediately asked the FTC to demand that Intel recall the chips. With protests escalating and an impending boycott threat, Intel conceded to modify the chips so that the serial number was disabled unless a user turned it on. Even this solution did not satisfy Intel's critics, who pointed out that personal computer makers could easily remove the software patch that disables the serial number and ship their products with the serial numbers turned on. Others worried that intruders could still break into a system and turn on the switch.

There is no question that the Intel serial number would enhance the security of on-line commercial transactions and help prevent fraud or theft of personal information. However, the tradeoff is the potential for a significant loss of privacy. Like the identifying mechanism of cookies, this architecture could also enable Web marketers to clandestinely track consumers on the Web by retrieving that serial number. Although Intel has disavowed any intention to build a master database of customer names linked to serial numbers, who knows what the future could bring.

Digital identification hard-wired into machines epitomizes the new authenticating architectures of cyberspace, which will verify identity, but also allow the identified user to be tracked on-line without consent or knowledge. Once again, we realize how technology makes it possible to raise monitoring and profiling to a new and more disturbing level.

Is it possible, however, to fight fire with fire, to use architectures that protect privacy rather than put it in harm's way? Can code be used to constrain the activities of those who are so anxious to exploit consumer information?

One such architecture that has promise is known as the *Platform for Privacy Preferences Project*, or *P3P*, developed by the World Wide Web Consortium (W3C). P3P provides a technological framework for users to negotiate with Web sites about what kinds of information they will disclose and how that information will be handled. It works something like this: the user enters personal information into his or her Web browser and describes the conditions under which he or she is willing to disclose this information—for example, information will be transmitted to a Web site provided that it is not sold to a third party. While surfing the Web, the user encounters a Web site collecting information: if the Web site has a policy that obeys the user's conditions, the personal information is automatically sent to that Web site; but if the Web site collects information under different conditions the browser warns the user and requests permission to convey the personal information, and unless that permission is granted, connection with the Web site will be terminated. Participating Web sites have a machine-readable proposal that can be automatically parsed by the user's agent, that is, normally the Web browser. Here is the proposal for an on-line company called Cool Catalog:

We collect click stream data in our HTTP logs. We also collect your first name, age and gender to customize our catalog pages for the type of clothing you are likely to be interested in and for our own research and product development. We do not use this information in a personally identifiable way. We do not redistribute this information outside of our organization. We do not provide access capabilities to information we may have from you, but we do have retention and opt-out policies, which you can read at our privacy page http://CoolCatalog.com/Privacy/Practice.html. The third party PrivacySeal.org provides assurance that we abide by this agreement.[20]

P3P is still in its experimental stage, but it does represent one way in which Internet architectures can be used to automatically protect consumers from giving out their information in a context that they have predefined as unsuitable. Despite several drawbacks, such as its complexity, P3P has numerous advantages. Users can establish one-to-one relationships with various Web sites and provide different amounts of data to each one depending on their policies. Users can also make exceptions based on the services provided by a particular Web site. Finally, users' information may be transferred automatically, thereby eliminating the need to key it in repeatedly.

P3P is certainly not a privacy panacea but it represents the first generation of technological tools that give the user control over how he or she wants to divulge personal data. If it becomes widely adopted and is further enhanced, it could play a moderate role in helping consumers retrieve their privacy.

## ▶ Searching for Solutions

Can the privacy problem be satisfactorily resolved? Can the situation be reversed so that some sensitive information remains shielded from public view? Now that all of this information is an on-line commodity, any reversal of these trends will be exceedingly difficult. Nonetheless, there may be measures that should be taken to limit the damage and perhaps protect classes of sensitive data such as one's medical background. Which combination of constraints—that is, norms, free market forces, regulation, or technology—will provide an optimal solution to this problem?

Two basic options for protecting privacy exist. The first is government regulation, primarily through the constraint of law, which we find in countries like Europe. The second is reliance on self-regulation through a combination of constraints, including the market, norms, and technology. Data collectors and other custodians of information are responsible for developing reasonable privacy policies; they may be guided by informal and voluntary standards established by industry trade groups such as the Direct Marketing Association or even by government agencies.

Let's turn first to government regulation. There are several possible regulatory models. For example, the government could mandate some type of *informed consent*. Vendors would be required by law to seek permission or consent before selling or reusing someone's personal information. There are two variations of this model. The first is the *"opt-in"* approach whereby individuals must explicitly approve secondary uses of their personal information. For example, if one provides credit data to a bank to apply for a loan, the bank cannot sell that data to a marketing company without permission. The second is the *"opt-out"* approach whereby individuals are notified that their personal data will be used for secondary purposes unless they disapprove and notify the vendor accordingly. If informed consent is to work properly, regulations would need to ensure that consumers have *knowledge and opportunity;* that is, users must be made aware of any projected reuse in a timely fashion and be given a reasonable opportunity to restrict it.

The government could also change the rules about information ownership. After all, who really owns credit, medical, or other data generated about individuals? The current laws are ambiguous, and consequently, most organizations that gather this information have assumed such ownership. However, it is by no means evident that the activity of data collection automatically engenders any property rights. But who deserves the most legitimate ownership claim on this data?

A controversial paradigm suggested by several scholars regards an individual's personal information as his or her private property. According to this paradigm, individuals should have property rights in all personal information about themselves, especially because they have the greatest stake in how that information will be used. If our information really has economic value, we should receive something in return when a corporation makes some profit from its reuse. By giving individuals such property rights, society recognizes both the economic value and the proprietary nature of personal information.

Once information is regarded as personal property, as an asset with legal attributes, the legal system can begin to develop a set of laws and appropriate regulations that will define when information should be protected from misappropriation, how individuals should be compensated when their information is used by a third party, and when information must be relinquished for the sake of social, public policy, or even technological priorities. Property rights are not absolute, and just as one's physical property may be subject in extreme cases to eminent domain, one's personal information must at times be sacrificed for the common good.

Although this approach may be theoretically sound, it unfortunately entails a plethora of practical problems. Users would be forced to negotiate with every vendor or Web-based business seeking their information. This would have a debilitating effect on the free flow of commercial data, and it would also be a time-consuming burden for both parties.

Those who advocate the need for privacy legislation to protect consumers in on-line transactions point to the poor track record of industries that have adopted some type of self-regulation. They are skeptical that business will have the moral discipline needed to police itself. In their view, only federal legislation establishing uniform national privacy standards will be sufficient to protect consumer privacy. Furthermore, they point out that the regulatory model has been effective in many European countries.

The second approach is to trust organizations that collect and disseminate personal data to impose constraints upon themselves to avoid infringing upon an individual's privacy rights. The motivation for imposing these constraints can come from several sources, such as market pressures or simply a respect for the principle of privacy rights.

The "invisible hand" of the market sometimes does compel companies to abide by certain moral norms for purely pragmatic reasons, but is this likely to happen with privacy rights? If privacy is important to consumers, some vendors may eventually come to recognize this by making promises of confidentiality. This will enhance the confidence and trust of their customers. Therefore, the demands of consumers and competitive pressures might force businesses to establish stronger privacy and security standards. A commitment to confidentiality and tight security may mean higher prices, but consumers who care about their privacy will not balk at paying a premium for this privilege. This may be especially true in cyberspace, where e-commerce has not reached its full potential because of lingering concerns over privacy protection. Some consumers may be willing to pay a bit extra for ironclad guarantees of security and confidentiality in their on-line transactions.

It seems highly unlikely, however, that free market mechanisms alone can significantly reverse the trend of privacy erosion. Some businesses will attempt to take advantage of privacy concerns through opportunistic marketing, but the payoffs and marketing benefits of trading in the commodity of information are too great to rely on market forces to bring under control predatory information collection practices.

Companies could also regulate themselves for other motives. They may seek to pre-empt government regulations, which they fear could be more onerous than their own self-imposed constraints. Or they may have purer motives and be convinced that privacy standards deserve their respect and that they should act with ethical probity. In all probability, if self-regulation works, it will be for reasons based on some combination of these different motives.

Some U.S. trade organizations, such as the powerful Direct Marketing Association (DMA), have long advocated this approach and have developed privacy principles for its members. These principles require that on-line companies post and follow privacy policies telling consumers how information about them will be used. The DMA has a seal of approval for Web sites that have a track record of fidelity to these principles.

Finally, we must not overlook a third possibility, a more bottoms-up approach that directly involves consumers in the safeguarding of their own privacy rights with the help of technology. In the absence of government regulation or consistent corporate self-regulation, consumers may take privacy matters into their own hands by adopting Internet architectures such as P3P and insisting that on-line businesses conform. Used properly, P3P and related architectures *could* have the potential to achieve the right balance between privacy rights and economic efficiency.

## ▶ A Prescription for Privacy

In Europe, comprehensive regulations imposed by the government will ensure that privacy is not left to the whims of the marketplace or the precariousness of self-regulation. In the United States, a more multifaceted and nuanced solution may be optimal for this complex problem. In situations in which confidentiality breaches could lead to serious harm, federal legislation may be essential. There are already laws that protect credit data (Fair Credit Reporting Act), and given the highly sensitive nature of medical information, government regulations will ultimately be necessary to protect that information as well. In determining which kinds of information deserve regulatory protection, the principle of proportionality should apply; that is, the need for government regulation should be commensurate with the potential for injury if the information is divulged inappropriately.

A tenable, but certainly debatable, case could be made that regular consumer data does not satisfy the principle of proportionality. A user's shopping profile is much less sensitive information than a medical or financial profile. Nonetheless, this data too deserves some measure of protection. One viable option that deserves consideration is reliance on mechanisms like P3P that hold great promise for privacy regulation without the need for a new legal framework. P3P is a way for the on-line industry to regulate itself through the discipline of technology. It recognizes implicitly that users have a property right in their information, and yet it does not require that the legal regime be overhauled to protect that right. Of course, all companies that operate on the Web have a deep moral duty to respect the value of privacy. Hence, in the absence of regulations, they should voluntarily embrace technologies like P3P as an ideal means of living up to that duty. They will be required to disclose their privacy policies openly and honestly in a statement like the one formulated by CoolCatalog. To work most effectively and to further ensure consumer confidence, P3P will also require self-auditing and monitoring by a third party, such as TRUSTe, that would take punitive action against those who violate their policies. Given the growing concerns that consumers have about privacy, it is also likely that the market will reward those on-line firms that do participate.

*Self-regulation facilitated by technology* seems to be one component of a comprehensive solution for safeguarding personal privacy. Technologies like P3P eliminate the need for individuals to negotiate with each Web site; instead, Web sites can transparently negotiate directly with users' computer systems. However, none of this will really work unless participating vendors truly respect the core value of privacy. Unless they approach this issue with the right attitude of moral sincerity, there will be temptations to look for loopholes or exploit shortcomings in the system. There is no substitute for organizational integrity, which breeds the conscientiousness and self-discipline that are essential for effective and durable self-regulation.

## ▶ Privacy in the Workplace

During the past two decades, technology has significantly redefined the nature of work as corporations and users rely more heavily on IT to process data and help control their far-scattered operations. IT has enabled many corporations to redesign the flow of work and to automate more routine processes. The Internet has clearly played a major role in all of this by expediting the interorganizational communication and data flows.

However, there is a more ominous side to this transformation of the workplace. Technology has also facilitated greater control over employees and a heightened intrusiveness into their private lives. Some omniscient employers, for example, check the whereabouts of their employees through electronic monitoring, maintain health surveillance data banks, and regularly check up on an employee's e-mail, voice mail, and Web-surfing habits. There is a real danger that the workplace is becoming a panopticon where workers' activities and interactions are transparent to the corporate hierarchy.

We cannot do justice to this crucial topic in this chapter so we will confine our analysis here to a single but representative issue: the employee's right to e-mail privacy. Do corporations have a moral perogative to inspect the e-mail of their workers or should employees be able to communicate via e-mail without the fear that their messages will be read by managers? Before we discuss this issue, some background on workplace privacy is in order.

Thanks in part to technological advancements and other pressures, we seem to be entering a new era in which there is a diminished respect for these workplace rights such as privacy. There appear to be several factors accounting for this change. Intense global competition and the exodus of American jobs to foreign countries with low labor costs have strengthened the position of many corporations while simultaneously weakening the bargaining leverage of once-powerful unions. In our more litigious society, there is also a greater threat of liability hanging over the corporate world. For example, corporations can now be held liable for negligent hiring if they fail to adequately check the background of their employees. And, of course, sophisticated surveillance technologies create the opportunity to exercise control in an unprecedented fashion. All of this has been especially perilous for privacy rights, which are not well protected in the law.

Although most organizations support the notion that their employees are entitled to some level of privacy protection, they have adopted policies that allow e-mail inspection. Employees are usually notified that their e-mail is not considered private and can be read at any time by their managers or by other authorized company officials. The core argument justifying this policy is simple: an e-mail network, including its contents, is owned by the employer, and hence the employer has a right to inspect these messages whenever it is deemed necessary. Employers contend that they have the right to read e-mail to make sure that employees are not using company property for private purposes. There is a conflict between the rights to ownership and privacy, and the employer claims that property rights should take precedence. Certainly, in countries such as the United States, there has been a tradition of supporting the right of property owners to monitor their property, so the employer is on pretty firm legal ground.

Those who support e-mail monitoring also point out that employers can be held liable for what their employees transmit over a corporate e-mail system, either to those within the company or to external parties. If an employer uses that system to harass his or her fellow employees, the company might be held legally liable if it can be demonstrated that they are too tardy in taking corrective actions; hence the need for careful and routine monitoring.

On the other hand, there are several convincing arguments supporting workplace privacy rights, including at least a *prima facie* e-mail privacy right. We will focus on one line of reasoning that seems especially pertinent. This argument centers on each person's fundamental right to autonomy, to make choices freely and direct one's activities. As we argued earlier in this chapter, privacy is a critical prerequisite for the exercise of one's autonomy. Without privacy, autonomy will be consistently threatened and enervated. Moreover, autonomy is a basic aspect of one's humanity according to moral common sense and most philosophical traditions. Thus, respect for the autonomy of others is a moral imperative that cannot be arbitrarily jettisoned or overridden for the sake of economic expediency. As Pat Werhane has argued, disrespecting the right to autonomy in the workplace "is equivalent to disrespecting employees as persons."[21] Because privacy is a necessary condition of autonomous behavior, it follows that workers must have some sort of privacy rights.

Of course, this does not imply that employees have complete freedom in the workplace environment because they are accountable to their employers for fulfilling the normal demands of their jobs. Autonomy and privacy must be circumscribed appropriately and circumspectly to help meet those demands. It does mean, however, that unless there is a *legitimate "need to know"* employers should not be gathering information about their employees that needlessly erodes their privacy and thereby threatens their basic autonomy.

Most employers would probably agree with all of this, at least from a theoretical point of view. They do not deny that their workers are entitled to *some* level of privacy protection. Most employers, for example, recognize that they should not spy on their workers at home or pry too deeply into the irrelevant details of their personal lives. However, their tendency is to acknowledge a narrow right to privacy, whereas civil libertarians would argue for a more robust right. There is also disagreement over the propriety of methods used to collect information about employees. Some corporations have used questionable methods, such as polygraph tests, psychological testing, and covert surveillance cameras, to acquire data about their workers.

Given these disagreements, how do we achieve a responsible equilibrium between workers' privacy rights and the corporation's need for information? There seems to be at least two important guidelines that can help us delineate the appropriate privacy zone for employees. First, employers should gather only *relevant* information about their employees. For prospective employees, this will undoubtedly include job history and other important background information; for employees already on the job, it will include data related to job performance or the furtherance of corporate objectives. Second, an employer should use only *ordinary* and common methods of acquiring information, that is, "the supervisory activities that are normally used to oversee employees' work."[22] Employers should not routinely use extraordinary data collection methods, which include the deployment of hidden surveillance devices, secret cameras, wiretaps, polygraph testing, and so forth. As Joseph DesJardins argues, extraordinary means of data collection, such as "blanket surveillance of all employees," are illegitimate because they are so intrusive and potentially harmful.[23] Hence they should not be adopted unless the circumstances themselves are extraordinary. For example, suspicion that trade secrets were being pilfered or that company property was being misused would certainly justify the use of extraordinary measures to ensure their protection. In some cases, certain extraordinary methods may also be necessary for quality control purposes.

Monitoring and reading e-mail in a systematic fashion is a form of surveillance and hence falls under the classification of extraordinary data collection methods. Robert Clarke defines *surveillance* as the "systematic investigation or monitoring of the actions or communications of one or more persons."[24] When a company's policy permits its managers to monitor and routinely read their employee's e-mail, that policy is promoting activities that are tantamount to surveillance.

Even if one concedes that monitoring e-mail is a form of surveillance and is an extraordinary means of inquiry into employee activities, it may not be immediately apparent that *this* type of surveillance is really impertinent or harmful. It is instructive to consider, therefore, precisely how the extraordinary data collection method of e-mail monitoring is an intrusive invasion of one's privacy.

Clearly, when one's e-mail messages are randomly inspected, one's privacy is violated because confidentiality (or secrecy) and anonymity are lost. Recall that these are two key elements of Ruth Gavison's definition of privacy. The information in the message is no longer confidential because it is read by a third party (a systems administrator or a manager) and the names of the sender and receiver are exposed, so both lose their anonymity.

But in what ways could this be officious and harmful? For example, many interactions in the workplace intersperse business and personal information; this often happens inadvertently when workers allude to certain aspects of their personal lives as they conduct business. It seems unfair and unrealistic to demand that workers refrain from doing this at all times. Also, employees who regularly work from 9 AM to 5 PM (and in many cases, for much longer hours) often have no choice but to conduct some personal business affairs from their offices. As a result, those companies that routinely inspect e-mail will sometimes become privy to an employee's business affairs or to sensitive details about an employee's personal life.

Furthermore, the loss of *anonymity* could be consequential in some situations. For example, the correspondence between two workers, Joe and Marie, might be perfectly innocuous and professional, but Marie's manager might draw an unwarranted inference from the frequency of those communications or it may be referenced out of context. This might affect her future position in the company.

Given the harm that can come to individuals through surveillance and this attendant loss of confidentiality and anonymity, many argue that employees deserve at least a *prima facie* or conditional e-mail privacy right. A presumption must be given to privacy rights instead of property rights because human dignity is at stake.

This dispute over e-mail privacy is fraught with many ambiguities and complexities, and it will probably never be resolved to the satisfaction of all the relevant stakeholders. As long as employers assert their property rights and as long as they worry about potential liabilities for what their employees do with the corporate e-mail system, they will be reluctant to recognize even a conditional right to e-mail privacy in the workplace.

## Discussion Questions

1. In your estimation, could self-regulation be effective in protecting data privacy or does it need to be supplemented by laws and regulations? Is the European model worth emulating?

2. What is your general assessment of cookie technology? Should there be some self-imposed limits on how this technology is used?
3. Is it morally acceptable for an employer to intercept the e-mail of its employees? Under what circumstances should an ISP be permitted to tap into the electronic communications of its users?

## CASE STUDY

### Using Cookies at greatcareers.com (Hypothetical)

You have just opened a new Web site called www.greatcareers.com. The purpose of this Web site is to be a clearing house of information for people looking for jobs, especially in the Boston and New York areas. Users can sign up for this site free of charge to look through the extensive job listings, which are displayed weekly. The major sections of the Web page are divided according to different fields of work and different professions.

Your projected source of revenues is primarily from the ads that display on each page. One advertising agency that supplies you with some of your advertisers requests to be provided with some "cookie" information of your subscribers. They intend to use the "cookie" information, which includes the user's search criteria, to generate a more personalized stream of ads for each user. Thus, individuals searching for teaching jobs would see different ads than someone looking for a nursing job. Such customized ads have the potential to generate more revenue.

This seems like a reasonable proposition, but you wonder whether it is legitimate to use cookie technology in this way. If so, should your users be informed about this practice? Should they be given an opportunity to "opt-out?"

#### Questions
1. Discuss the pros and cons of this proposal. What would you choose to do?
2. Is the principle of informed consent applicable here?

## CASE STUDY

### AOL and On-Line Privacy

Steve Case and other executives at America Online (AOL) were not prepared for the firestorm of controversy that greeted their latest press release. In that release, AOL verified that it was planning to sell the home phone numbers of their 8.5 million customers to selected telemarketers. Many AOL customers and even some government leaders called or e-mailed the company to register their dissatisfaction. In the wake of this strident protest, AOL needed to make some quick decisions.

Before their acknowledgment of this plan, AOL had signed deals with two marketing organizations: CUC International, a vendor of discount shopping services, and TelSave Holdings, Inc., a discount phone service. Apparently, AOL planned to give these two companies the phone numbers of their customers so that they could follow up with targeted telemarketing calls.

This was the second time in less than six months that AOL, America's largest on-line service provider, found itself besieged with customer complaints. In January of 1997, AOL began offering a flat monthly fee of $19.95 in exchange for unlimited Internet access. However, the company failed to upgrade its network capacity to accommodate peak traffic. As a result, AOL could not handle the added volume generated by this promotion and it was forced to provide rebates to many irate subscribers. The company was just recovering from the ill-effects of this public relations debacle, and in the view of many outsiders, it could ill-afford another publicity setback.

As AOL executives read over some the more vehement complaints of their subscribers, they reflected upon their options. They could forge ahead with their plans or perhaps use their own employees to make the marketing phone calls on behalf of CUC International and TelSave. AOL had assembled a proficient telemarketing group within its organization to peddle goods such as the AOL Visa card to its customer base. Under this plan, their role would simply be expanded.

As the controversy intensified, AOL managers faced some difficult questions. Should it stick with its plans to disseminate the phone numbers of its on-line subscribers and hope that the negative attention would soon dissipate? Also, how should it deal with those subscribers who did not want to receive these calls?

## Questions

1. Recommend a specific course of action for AOL. Which philosophical or ethical principle underlies your position?
2. Should these phone numbers be off limits for AOL under any circumstances? Is the company violating their subscribers' privacy by making these calls?

## References

1. Quoted in Gleick, J. 1996. Big brother is us. *New York Times Magazine,* September 29, p. 130.
2. Gavison, R. 1984. Privacy and the limits of the law. *The Yale Law Journal* 89:421–471.

3. Reiman, J. 1995. Driving to the panopticon: A philosophical exploration of the risks to privacy posed by the highway technology of the future. *Santa Clara Computer and High Technology Law Journal* 11(1):27–44.
4. Gould, C. 1989.*The information Web: Ethical and social implications of computer networking.* Boulder, CO: Westview Press, p. 44.
5. Wassestrom, R. 1984. Privacy: Some arguments and assumptions. In Schoeman, F. (Ed.). *Philosophical dimensions of privacy.* New York: Cambridge University Press, p. 328.
6. Foucault, M. 1979. *Discipline and punish: The birth of the prison.* New York: Vintage Books, p. 200.
7. Moor, J. 1997. Towards a theory of privacy in the information age. *Computers and Society* September:29.
8. For a detailed account, see Bulkeley, W. M. 1998. Prescriptions, toll free numbers yield a gold mine for marketers. *The Wall Street Journal,* April 17, p. B1.
9. Deck, S. 1998. Sabre in privacy hotseat. *Computerworld,* July 13, p. 65.
10. Wasserman, E. 1998. Internet industry fails government's test. *The Industry Standard,* June 8, p. 19.
11. Gimein, M. 1998. The peculiar business of one-to-one marketing. *The Industry Standard,* August 24. p. 19.
12. *Children in cyberspace: A privacy resource guide.* Privacy Rights Clearinghouse (www. privacyrights.org).
13. See Seligman, D. 1998. Too much of a good thing. *Forbes,* February 28, pp. 64–65.
14. Singleton, S. 1998. *Privacy as censorship: A skeptical view of proposals to regulate privacy in the private sector.* Washington DC: Cato Institute. See www.cato.org.
15. Ibid.
16. Ibid.
17. Gandy, O. 1996. Coming to terms with the panoptic sort. In Lyon, D. (Ed.). *Computers, surveillance, & privacy.* Minneapolis: University of Minnesota Press, pp. 132–158.
18. Hance, O. 1996. *Business and law on the Internet.* New York: McGraw-Hill, p. 129.
19. Andrews, E. 1998. European law aims to protect privacy of data. *The New York Times,* October 26, p. A1.
20. See the CoolCatalog Web page at http://www.CoolCatalog.com/catalogue.
21. Werhane, P. 1985. *Persons, rights and corporations.* Englewood Cliffs, NJ: Prentice Hall, p. 103.
22. Velasquez, M. 1992. *Business ethics: Concepts and cases* (3rd ed). Englewood Cliffs, NJ: Prentice Hall, p. 400.
23. Des Jardins, J. 1985. *Contemporary issues in business ethics.* Belmont, CA: Wadsworth, p. 226.
24. Clarke, R. 1988. Information technology and dataveillance. *Communications of the ACM* May:499.

# CHAPTER SIX

# Securing the Electronic Frontier

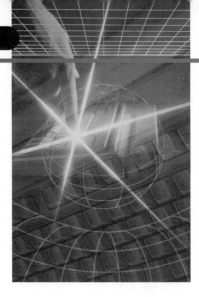

## ▶ Introduction

If there is any obstacle to the explosive growth of the Internet, it has to be the public's apprehension about its security flaws. Stories often appear in the press exposing new problems and underscoring the Internet's fragile infrastructure. Despite the use of fire walls, security scanners, intrusion prevention products, and other security devices, Web sites have been the latest target for hackers. Hacking popular Web pages seems to be one of the most fashionable and costly forms of electronic intrusion. A recent PriceWaterhouseCoopers study revealed that 59% of all companies with Web sites experienced one or more security break-ins during 1997. Moreover, this figure is probably too low because many of these incidents usually go unreported.

One of the more notorious and widely publicized security breaches happened to *The New York Times* on September 13, 1998. Their Web site server was invaded by a group of belligerent hackers who posted pornographic material and printed this threatening message for all to see:

FIRST OFF, WE HAVE TO SAY . . . WE OWN YOUR DUMB ASS. S3COND, TH3R3 AR3 SO MANY LOS3ERS H3R3. ITZ HARD TO PICK WHICH TO INSULT THE MOST.

The site had to be closed for nine hours while information technology (IT) personnel cleaned up the offensive messages and plugged the hole.[1]

Of course, security breaches on the Internet can go well beyond attacks on a solitary commercial Web site. In testimony before Congress in May 1998, several current and former hackers, members of a watch-dog group called Lopht Heavy Industries, boasted that they would have no trouble in bringing the Internet to its knees in less than 30 minutes! They asserted that the Internet is so vulnerable that "it would be possible to terminate communications between the United States and all other countries and to prevent major backbone providers such as MCI and AT&T from routing network traffic to each other."[2] The group agreed to testify out of concern that business and government officials are too naive and nonchalant about security matters. According to these hackers, these officials do not seem to appreciate the risks associated with managing 'net-centric organizations. One hopes that this group's worst fears will never be realized. However, the Internet's insecurity may prove to have devastating consequences one day, and yet this issue still does not receive the serious attention and the financial support it deserves.

One of the first cases that brought the public's attention to the Internet's vulnerable infrastructure was the "Internet Worm," developed by Robert Morris, a student at Cornell University. In November 1988, Morris released a worm, a concise, self-replicating C program, from Cornell's host computer system so that it would quickly spread to other systems on the Internet. This worm's progress was facilitated by a fatal security flaw in the UNIX operating system software of the infected machines. Once these computers were invaded, the program reproduced itself incessantly, consuming large volumes of memory. It did not modify system files or destroy any information, but the performance of systems infected by the "worm" deteriorated rapidly, causing many of them to crash.

Approximately 12 hours after the first system was infected, the Computer Systems Research Group at Berkeley developed a program to halt the worm's rapid spread. All of these disabled computer systems had to be taken off-line in order to apply the remedial and preventive measures necessary to destroy the worm and prevent its recurrence. The final toll: 2,000 computers infected in some way and a clean up cost of more than $1 million.[3]

Fortunately, incidents on this scale are not that common, but in the years since this event occurred, it does not appear that enough progress has been made in securing the electronic frontier. As more and more organizations begin heavily relying on the Internet for electronic commerce (e-commerce) or other networking applications, they are discovering the complexity of securing their systems. The fundamental problem is familiar: the 'net's architecture is radically open, designed to share information and not to conceal it. It is possible to develop an adequate level of security with an acceptable degree of risk, but this requires an investment of time and money that many government agencies and corporations have been reluctant to make.

There are many dimensions to the broad issue of Internet security. Security threats include viruses, time bombs, worms, unauthorized access, on-line theft, and so on. Although there are defensive mechanisms that protect computer systems from these electronic invasions or other attacks, no system is impregnable. Hackers have also proven to be adept in locating and exploiting even the smallest security vulnerabilities.

This chapter dwells on just three basic issues that are intimately connected with some of the other themes that have been articulated in this book. We first examine the issue of "trespass," or unauthorized access, perhaps the most common and persistent security problem on the Internet. Trespass may seem like a simple matter, but it is characterized by some unusual ethical and legal ambiguities. Is this even the appropriate metaphor for electronic intrusion? What constitutes trespass in cyberspace? Why is it so wrong even if no damage is done, and what are the appropriate legal remedies for its victims?

Second, we devote some attention to the matter of encryption and the public policy debate it has generated. One way to achieve information security is by encrypting one's electronic communications. This makes the data unreadable to anyone who does not have a key to the encrypted data. However, the U.S. government has sought some control over this technology because it fears that in the hands of criminals and terrorists, encryption can be used to develop unbreakable codes. However, there is no denying that handing over the keys to the government amounts to a setback for privacy rights.

What is at issue then is a challenging question: do users have a right to privacy and the confidentiality of their data communications that takes priority over the national security interests of a legitimate government? After we provide some background on the twists and turns of the prolonged encryption controversy, we attempt to do justice to that provocative question.

Finally, we review the most salient security threats to e-commerce. This discussion includes some treatment of various measures that can be taken to secure on-line commercial transactions such as the use of digital certificates and other protocols that are designed to safeguard the integrity of information being transmitted to and from Web sites.

Our purpose here is not to provide an exhaustive account of the Internet's security flaws or a primer about proper preventive measures. Rather, the purpose is to explore the ethical dimension of this important problem, to illustrate how the critical goal of information security can sometimes collide with other worthy objectives, and to ponder how these competing objectives can be effectively balanced.

## ▶ Trespass in Cyberspace

### Cybertrespassing as a Moral Problem

Unauthorized access to computer systems is a widespread problem on the Internet. Despite the efforts of legal authorities to clamp down on cyberspace trespassers, there is still an unfortunate tendency to avoid taking these transgressions all that seriously. The culprits are often recreational hackers who thrive on breaking into supposedly "secure" systems. Indeed, according to Dorothy Denning, the hacker ethic is predicated on this basic principle: "Access to computers—and anything which might teach you something about the way the world works—should be unlimited and total."[4]

As far back as 1983, when Neil Patrick and six other Milwaukee teenagers were convicted of computer trespassing, their response was that "we were just playing a game." But the so-called game involved alleged breaking into institutions with extremely sensitive data, such as the Los Alamos National Laboratory and the Sloan Kettering Cancer Center in New York. And consider the advertising for the popular Hollywood movie *Hackers,* which proclaimed "Their only crime was curiosity." The message implicit in both the advertising and the movie itself was that these high school computer nerds really hadn't done anything so terribly wrong by breaking into secured computer systems all over the United States. Unfortunately, this movie typifies the distorted perspective of the media, which has sometimes tended to sensationalize hacking and to elevate hackers to celebrity status.

The problem is that many people do not see an exact parallel between trespassing on a computer system and physically trespassing on somebody's property. They regard the former as more abstract, rationalizing that networked computer systems are something to be "borrowed" and returned with no harm done. But is unauthorized access the same as physical trespass despite the fact that the Internet's architecture is such an open and unstructured environment?

Even if one answers this question affirmatively, the notion of trespass in cyberspace still raises some intriguing questions, partly because of the lack of physical boundaries. For example, if someone releases a worm or virus, does that virus trespass on the computer system that it infects? Is unsolicited e-mail or spam a form of trespass, especially if it is forced upon another's e-mail inbox, which is part of that individual's personal space? Or does linking to other Web sites without permission constitute trespassing? If these actions do rise to the legal bar of trespass, it will give their victims another source of remedy because trespassing is a criminal offense.

The Computer Fraud and Abuse Act (CFAA), which was last amended in late 1996, is evidence that the U.S. legal system has begun to take this issue more seriously. The provisions of the Act protect the confidentiality of proprietary information and make it a crime to "knowingly access a computer without or in excess of authority to obtain classified information." The statute also makes it a crime to access any "protected computer" without authorization and as a result of such access to defraud victims of property or to recklessly cause damage. Protected computers include those used by the government, financial institutions, or any business engaged in interstate or international commerce. Thus, trespass is a federal crime if one does so to pilfer classified information, to perpetrate fraud, or to cause damage (for example, to destroy files or disable an operating system). The only strict trespass provision of the statute protects computers used on a full-time or part-time basis by the government from unauthorized access, even if no damage is done and no information is stolen.[5]

All of the states, with the exception of Vermont, have also enacted their own computer crime statutes, which, in some cases, go beyond the scope of the Computer Fraud and Abuse Act. Specifically, most state laws make unauthorized use of computers a crime regardless of the circumstances.

Some have argued that law enforcement officials should not be taking such a hard line against purely recreational hacking, that is, incidents of trespassing that do not involve damage to property or data theft. Numerous arguments have been put forth to defend break-ins by hackers, especially when there is no deliberate destruction of property. Among these arguments, we find the following: break-ins actually serve a valuable purpose because they uncover security flaws that would otherwise go unnoticed, and the intruder is probably using only idle resources, so there is really no cost for the victim. There is also what Eugene Spafford calls the student hacker argument—"some trespassers claim that they are doing no harm and changing nothing—they are simply learning about how computer systems operate."[6] Still others might say that a little digital graffiti on a World Wide Web site is merely a prank and should be treated accordingly.

On the surface, it might appear that some of these arguments are plausible and that there is little or no harm to most forms of electronic intrusion. For example, if a hacker is able to penetrate a secure environment and search through a few programs but does no damage, where is the harm? This might be analogous to walking through someone's property while leaving everything perfectly in tact. Thus, one could argue that unauthorized access that leaves the environment undisturbed is only a minor ethical transgression and not worth much of a fuss. And digital graffiti is not much worse because it can be cleaned up more easily than the graffiti that comes from spray paint.

If we examine the problem through the lens of Lessig's framework, it is apparent that the strongest constraints on this deviant behavior are technology and the law. Numerous technologies have been designed to deter hackers, as well as laws such as the CFAA that prescribe strict punishment for electronic trespassing. On the other hand, social norms are ambivalent because we do find some cultural acceptance of hacking in cyberspace. Society sends mixed signals about hackers who are seen as rogues and villains but also as modern-day Robin Hoods and adventurers, who deserve some credit for their skill and ingenuity.

This ambivalence is not found, however, when we apply ethical standards to hacking. To begin with, it is generally recognized that it is simply wrong to trespass, even if no direct damage is caused. *When one trespasses, one violates respect for property rights, which is an important ethical and social value.* Property rights buttress the moral good of autonomy because they allow individuals to control what they own, which is essential for their commercial and personal well-being. Breaking into a private corporate headquarters after hours just to look around the lobby is still trespassing, even if one does not pilfer any files or cause any damage. There is no basis to treat a hacker who breaks into a secured computer site only to "look around" any differently. Individuals should not go where they do not belong, either in real space or in cyberspace—this is a fundamental rule of law and basic tenet of morality.

Furthermore, the hacker may intrude into a system and not intend to do any harm, but he or she may inadvertently damage a file or program. The more complex the system, the more likely the occurrence of accidental damage. In addition, unauthorized use of a computer system wastes the victim's valuable CPU resources, which amounts to a more tangible form of theft. Moreover, even if there is no malicious intent or destruction of Web pages, a trespasser's activities can still be disruptive and costly because any unwarranted intrusion must be inspected by system administrators. They must spend time verifying and checking their systems and software to make sure that no damage has been done. Finally, as Deborah Johnson points out, "those who attempt to gain unauthorized access, plant worms and viruses, and so on, force the computing community to put energies and resources into protecting systems and files when they could be using their energy and resources to improve the technology in other ways."[7]

Thus, as Spafford and others have illustrated, most of the arguments that support hackers are spurious ones that do not stand up to objective scrutiny. The case against hacking is even stronger when property is stolen or Web pages are defaced because greater harm is inflicted upon the victim, who must expend even more resources to fix these problems.

## Trespass and Web Sites

There are two ways in which property rights of Web site owners can be transgressed. The first occurs when the Web page is hacked by intruders.

The content is usually damaged by adding files to the Web server. The second is much less serious but certainly not inconsequential, and it involves unauthorized visits to a Web page. This might take place if one cracks a password code to an on-line seminar and participates without permission. Although most Web sites are open to the general public, some are accessible only to authorized users and require a password and username before entry. In rare cases, Web site owners have limited access to their sites by means of the honor system. Several law firms, for example, indicate on their home pages that anyone may browse through their sites as long as they are not using a commercial computer service that charges for every minute of use. Those who defied this instruction and continued reading would technically be guilty of trespassing.

If any of these acts *are* equivalent to trespass, the implication is that Web sites are property. Property is usually understood to be physical property or chattel of some sort. But does a Web site also qualify as real private property? Despite the fact that the World Wide Web is an open and public environment where users are invited to participate, the notion that a Web site is the property of its owner does have some plausibility.

Trotter Hardy relies on some of the familiar philosophical arguments we invoked in Chapter Four to demonstrate that a Web site should indeed be classified as property. As a result, both unwanted visitors and Web page hackers are culpable of trespassing. He cites Locke's "labor-desert" theory and utilitarianism to justify his claim. From a Lockean perspective, there ought to be property rights in Web sites because "their value and even their existence derive entirely from someone else's labor in setting up the site."[8] The production of a Web site is often a labor-intensive activity, and this effort should confer a property right for those who made the investment of time and effort to build that site. Likewise, the utilitarian argument that ownership rights are justified because they maximize social utility and provide an incentive to build future Web sites is less compelling but still somewhat germane. To some extent, a recognition of private property rights in a Web site does provide an incentive to develop new sites because developers will realize that they will retain firm control over the accessibility to these sites.

Therefore, Hardy concludes that a common law "cause of action for 'trespass to Web sites' should exist as a means of controlling access to Web sites."[9] Although Web page hacking is the more serious offense, users must respect Web sites that are off limits as long as a Web site properly signals the restriction. Right now, almost all Web site owners encourage visitors, and this is as it should be. The Internet should be a public place, an open forum for the exchange of ideas and information. The common good of Internet users is clearly advanced by such open access. That does not imply, however, that Web sites are public property, fair game for users and hackers.

As the World Wide Web continues its phenomenal expansion, it is hard to predict whether there will be many more proprietary Web sites that will restrict or limit access. Our point is that the institution of private property and the common law of trespass do have relevance in cases of unauthorized access to such sites. Furthermore, although we must encourage an open World Wide Web that does not impede a user's navigation or constrain information flows, there is a strong moral imperative to respect the property boundaries of a Web server and the Web pages that it generates.

## Spam as Trespass?

Before we move on to other matters, it would be instructive to revisit the issue of spam. As we discussed in Chapter Three, spam has imposed significant costs on its recipients and especially on the Internet Service Providers (ISPs) that serve as a medium for the spammer. Some ISPs have retaliated by suing spammers for trespass to personal property, and they have sought injunctive relief to protect that property.

The property issue as it relates to spam is somewhat complicated. Spam is transmitted from the sender through a mail server, where it may reside for some time before it is sent on to the recipient. Therefore, spam affects both the property of the ISP, which owns and operates the mail server, and the property of the final recipient.

The case of *CompuServe Incorporated v. CyberPromotions, Inc.,* is indicative of the ambiguities and challenges raised by the claim that spam transmitted through an ISP violates property rights. The case was triggered when CompuServe notified CyberPromotions that it was prohibited from using its mail servers to transmit unsolicited advertisements. CyberPromotions refused to comply, and CompuServe filed suit contending that the defendant was trespassing on its property. CyberPromotions argued that because CompuServe invited others to enter its property for business purposes, it could not later restrict access to that property. In other words, when CompuServe put its mail server on the Internet, implicit permission was granted for any of its paying customers to use that server. They also argued that CompuServe had assumed the role of postmaster, to whom all the strictures of the First Amendment apply, and that to allow CompuServe to enjoy a legally protected interest in its computer equipment in this context is to license a form of censorship, which violates the First Amendment.

In a decision handed down in February 1997, Judge Graham of the U.S. District Court in Ohio ruled against CyberPromotions, rejecting its claims as groundless. Judge Graham fully recognized the burdens imposed by spam on mail servers and concluded that "the property rights of the private owner could not be overwhelmed by the First Amendment."[10] Moreover, reasoned the judge, because CompuServe is a private actor and not a government agency seeking to stifle CyberPromotion's right to communicate and because it is the owner of the computer property on which the transgression occurred, the defendant's defiant act does constitute trespass. As a result, it granted a preliminary injunction prohibiting CyberPromotions from sending unsolicited ads to any e-mail addresses maintained by CompuServe.

It is difficult to find fault with the Court's reasoning in this case. The decision to side with this ISP was clearly based on an analogy to physical trespass, which seems to fit here. What makes the case somewhat easy to resolve is that CompuServe's physical computer systems and disk drives were being used by CyberPromotions to send messages at a significant cost to CompuServe.

Recall that one of the elements in the definition of property is the right to exclude others from use. A corollary of that right is the need to seek permission of the owner to use his or her property. CyberPromotions assumed that it had permission to use CompuServe's mail servers without any restrictions. CompuServe, however, grants "permission" to use its mail servers with a caveat: one cannot overwhelm the mail server and thereby debilitate the system. Because it is an autonomous moral agent, it would seem that CompuServe has every moral and legal right to impose such a reasonable restriction on its users.

However, this case leaves unanswered a larger question that concerns the ultimate target of spam: does spam constitute trespass at the user level as well? If a company sends me unsolicited, unwanted e-mail, are they trespassing on my property? This is a much more complicated question and deserves further elaboration.

Some antispammers have asserted that all Internet communications should be consensual. This is an extreme position that would be difficult to justify from any ethical or practical standpoint. The heavy costs of such an exclusionary policy would far outweigh any benefits. Do most Internet users really want to preclude any communications to which they have not given their consent? Wouldn't they be impoverished by such a restriction? The open communications and democratic expression enabled by the Internet would be seriously undermined if we insisted that all exchanges had to be consensual.

Furthermore, the right to free speech is sufficiently broad in most countries to include the right to commercial speech. This implies that vendors and other organizations should have the right to send their promotional material to prospective on-line customers just as they have a right to send out advertisements and flyers through the regular mail.

However, although advertisers do have a right to send this mail, they do not have a right to force it on someone. If that were to occur, spam could rightfully be construed as a form of trespass. The right to communicate must be balanced with the rights of property and privacy, that is, the right to be left alone within one's own personal domain. To effect some compromise in this situation, individuals must be allowed to maintain some measure of control over this unwanted mail. Each individual should have the right to control his or her domain or private space. This should include the prerogative to protect it from unwanted mail, whether it be regular mail sent to one's house or e-mail sent to one's electronic mailboxes, which should also be regarded as an extension of one's private space or property. This is derived from the more basic right of autonomy over one's person and possessions, which is violated by the coercive activity of making someone a captive audience to another's communications. Of course, the user can exercise control simply by deleting the unwanted message. It also seems reasonable, however, that the user should be able to go a step further and tell the sender to stop sending any more messages or mailings. Failure to comply with that request would constitute trespassing on one's personal space. The right to communicate must be limited by the preferences of an unreceptive consumer. At a minimum, unsolicited e-mail amounts to trespassing when it is forced on individuals against their will.

Other aspects of trespass in cyberspace might bear some scrutiny as well, but they would also bring us into areas of legal complexity best left for another occasion. We have merely sought to provide an overview of this issue and, in so doing, to give the reader some idea of the challenges involved in determining when and if such trespass has occurred.

## ▶ The Encryption Controversy: A Public Policy Perspective

### Encryption on the 'Net

As we have already seen, the optimal means of achieving the elusive goal of information security is through the use of encryption. This technology enables users to transmit sensitive data over an insecure network like the Internet. Most Internet communications are vulnerable to eavesdroppers and saboteurs unless they are protected by encryption. The basic problem is that the Internet transmits information as if it were a postcard. A postcard is openly available for inspection by any snoops who care to see what it says. Likewise, as an e-mail message or other communication passes through various servers, it could be intercepted and read by system administrators or even unsophisticated hackers. Encryption prevents this by scrambling the data, making it impossible to read without the right key.

In this section, we consider the highly contentious issues revolving around the use of public key encryption. We provide some background material on cryptography itself and the nature of public key encryption and then review the history of the public policy proposals on encryption.

We conclude with some reflections on the ethical aspects of this technology and the proper role of government.

The term *cryptography* generally refers to data encryption, which is nothing more than a secret code. These codes have been used by the military for thousands of years. Cryptography works by taking an intelligible message, such as "we will invade tomorrow," and translating it into some sort of unintelligible gibberish. The only way that this gibberish can be translated into something meaningful is by means of a key. For example, the key used by the Roman conqueror Julius Caesar was the replacement of a letter by the letter that was three places ahead of it in the alphabet (thus the letter *d* would be replaced by the letter *g*). With the aid of this key, messages could be easily decrypted and rendered intelligible.

Computer cryptography or encryption has been in widespread use since the 1960s. Although numerous encryption algorithms have been developed, the most popular commercial one is the DES, or Data Encryption Standard, which the government has used as its standard since 1977. The DES was originally created in the 1960s by IBM researchers, but it was modified by the National Security Agency (NSA) before being adopted as a standard. In addition, there is the RSA, or Rivest-Shamir-Adelman, algorithm that was created by the three individuals at MIT with these surnames. The DES is currently used in many e-mail and networking packages and was recently recertified by the government in 1993.

The DES is a symmetric private key cryptography system; this simply means that the same secret binary key is used for both encryption and decryption. For this to work properly, both parties, the sender and receiver of the data, must have access to this key. The key itself then must be communicated in a secure fashion, or it could be intercepted by a third party and otherwise fall into the wrong hands. This is a serious disadvantage of the private key scheme.

The other popular encryption technique, RSA, is based on a public key cryptography. Public key encryption also enables a user to transmit data securely over unsecured networks. Each party gets a pair of keys, one public and one private; the public key is usually kept in a directory and is used to encrypt a message, and a secretive private key is used to decrypt the message.

The longer the key, the harder it is to be cracked; a 128-bit key would be almost impossible to crack, whereas a 40-bit key could be cracked pretty easily. In 1996, a group of cryptographers recommended that keys be at least 75 to 90 bits long "to protect against a well funded adversary."[11]

The obvious advantage of public key cryptography is that the sender and receiver of the message do not have to exchange a secret private key before they begin to communicate. The bottom line, according to Michael Baum, "is that public-key encryption creates trusted commerce for all parties doing business."[12]

However, public key encryption has been a problematic means of achieving "trusted commerce" thanks to the reluctance of government regulators to support this technology. The government is apprehensive about the export of sophisticated encryption systems (for example, 128-bit keys) and has been asking for "back door access," that is, some form of control over all public and private keys. It worries that international terrorists or bands of criminals will get their hands on an encryption system to which law enforcement authorities do not have the key and that cannot be decoded. Therefore, it is concerned that the proliferation of these systems will diminish its capacity for wire taps and surveillance and perhaps in the long run imperil national security. There are currently no restrictions on the domestic uses of encryption, but the U.S. federal government does restrict the export of encryption systems. The government has allowed exporting cryptographic software with 40-bit keys, which will protect a user against the casual cybersnooper but can be cracked easily by professionals. It has, however, steadfastly resisted the exports of high-end encryption systems unless a back door entry is provided.

Giving the government the key to all encryption systems has not been well received by privacy advocates or by the software industry because it seems to be too obtrusive and conjures up certain Orwellian overtones. Over the past few years, the government has offered a number of proposals to resolve this problem and deal with the tensions between preserving personal privacy while not compromising national security. It is instructive to review these proposals along with the criticisms that they have provoked.

## Public Policy Proposals on Encryption

### The Clipper Chip

The Clipper system, which was developed by the NSA, was designed especially for the encryption of telephone communications. The Clipper Chip itself is a microprocessor with an encoded algorithm known as Skipjack that was to be installed in every telephone. When two individuals using phones equipped with these Clipper Chip encryption devices decide that they want to secure their communications, they activate those devices to exchange a packet of information called a *LEAF* (Law Enforcement Access Field). The LEAF includes a special session key, which allows the callers to encode and decode the contents of the phone call. The LEAF also includes the chip's serial numbers. The FBI would have a universal family key that would decode the serial number but not the session key. When the FBI was granted a legal warrant to wiretap, it could then extract from the LEAF the serial numbers of the clipper chips in use.

As part of this plan, the government would maintain in escrow the master key to each Clipper Chip. The proposal was to have these unique numeric keys divided between two government agencies that would effectively act as custodial agents. One agency would hold one half of a key, and the other agency would hold the other half. Once the FBI has the proper serial number, they can request the two portions of the unique key from the respective government agencies holding them in escrow; each agency looks up the serial number provided by the FBI and provides its portion of the key corresponding to that number. The FBI combines the two halves of the key, enabling it to decode the session key in the LEAF along with the contents of the encrypted call.

The Clipper Chip proposal engendered enormous criticism and touched off a divisive debate. Security experts were quick to point out its many technical flaws: the Skipjack algorithm was classified, and the scrambling was done by circuits hard-wired on a tamper-proof computer chip rather than by software. This would make it more difficult to change or upgrade this technology in the future. It also has the effect of making products with these devices more expensive because tailor-made chips are costly. Finally, phones with these chips would not work with other phones.

But most of the criticism was based on ideology and not on the absence of sound technology. Many believed that key escrow plans like Clipper Chip are flawed because they rely on "trusted" third parties, and the more parties involved in a cryptography scheme, the weaker it is. Civil libertarians saw this "scheme" as a massive assault on privacy rights and raised the spectre of government officials routinely prying into the affairs of private citizens. John Perry Barlow's polemic against the Clipper Chip sounds like a call to arms:

> Clipper is a last ditch attempt by the United States, the last great power from the old Industrial Era, to establish imperial control over cyberspace. If they win, the most liberating development in the history of humankind could become, instead, the surveillance system which will monitor our grandchildren's morality. We can be better ancestors than that.[13]

The Clipper did have its supporters who feared what might happen if wiretapping became impossible because of hard-to-crack encryption technologies that didn't have any back doors. They appreciated the government's legitimate goal to prevent the spread of uncrackable encryption code. According to Stewart Baker, the strident and exaggerated opposition to Clipper reflected a "wide . . . streak of romantic high-tech anarchism that crops up throughout the computer world."[14]

To be sure, there is some merit to these arguments. The exploitation of encryption by terrorists or computer-literate criminals is a legitimate public safety issue. When the FBI recently broke up a child pornography network, it had to contend with encrypted computer files. Encryption was also a factor in the covert communications about the assassination attempt on Pope John Paul II. As criminals become more heavily reliant on computer systems to plan and execute their crimes, they will most likely turn to encryption to conceal these illicit activities.

Rhetoric aside, however, Barlow and his colleagues also had a legitimate claim about the potential intrusiveness of the Clipper Chip. In its efforts to balance national security needs and privacy, this technology put too much emphasis on national security by creating a system in which the risks to privacy invasions were unacceptably and unnecessarily high.

### Export Controls

As a result of this overwhelming criticism and steady negative publicity, the original Clipper Chip proposal was soon defunct and the government responded with a new version of regulations for data encryption in the fall of 1995. This scheme would permit the export of products with strong algorithms up to a 56-bit DES, but the government still wanted back-door access; as a result "spare keys" to those locks would have to be put in escrow and made available on demand to law enforcement agencies. Agencies who sought the escrowed keys would have to follow the same procedures used to get a wiretap. This proposal was seen as less intrusive than the ill-fated Clipper Chip, but it too failed to win industry support because there was widespread sentiment that 56-bit DES was inadequate. Also, privacy advocates were still uneasy about giving any government agency the key to these communications no matter what safeguards against abuse were put in place.

In May 1996, the National Research Council (NRC) issued a major report on this complex issue titled "Cryptography's Role in Securing the Information Society." The report argued that the export control should gradually be relaxed but not completely eliminated, that the federal government should drop export restrictions on encryption software already available abroad, and that the government should invest more heavily in programs to strengthen the FBI's and the CIA's ability to crack private encryption codes. It reasoned that those steps would improve communications security without jeopardizing confidentiality.

### Key Management Infrastructure

At the same time the NRC report was released, the government issued its third encryption plan in as many years: the Key Management Infrastructure (KMI). The NRC also authorized a government infrastructure with key recovery services. KMI was based on the premise that there must be a duly authorized certificate for all public keys. This would be achieved by registering the keys with a key escrow agent and having them digitally signed by certification authorities (CAs). These CAs would function as "digital notary's public" who would verify the identity of the individual associated with a given key. Certificates for public encryption keys would be issued only if the corresponding decryption keys were handed over to a key recovery agent. Both key escrow agents and certification authorities would be required to meet minimum security and performance standards.

Under this plan, encryption products with keys of any length could be exported as long as they included key escrow (which the government preferred to call key recovery), that is, as long as the organization had been issued the required certificate.

This proposal met with the same opposition from privacy advocates and software firms because the U.S. government would not abandon the requirement of key recovery. Some companies grew tired of waiting for the magic solution, however, and began working out compromises with the government. In early 1996, Lotus Development Corp. announced that it had won government approval to export a version of Notes 4.0 with high-end 64-bit encryption. It consented to giving a secret master key to the government so that law enforcement agencies could decode documents or messages encrypted in Notes. This meant that Lotus' foreign customers were vulnerable because their encrypted communications could be exposed to U.S. government officials without their knowledge. Lotus saw this as a compromise because it gave the government access to only 24 of the 64 bits. The government agreed to this because 40-bit keys are weak and can be cracked easily if necessary.

The KMI proposal also included some policy guidelines that were adopted in the fall of 1996. After considerable debate, the following changes were put into effect:

- Jurisdiction over cryptography exports would be shifted from the State Department to the Commerce Department.

- Companies could apply for approval to export encryption products using 56-bit DES with the proviso that they must present their plans to implement key recovery within a two-year period.

- Finally, high-end encryption products (such as 128-bit DES) could be exported but only if they included key recovery.

### Recent Developments

There has been a hodgepodge of proposed legislation for encryption regulations during the past two years, but the opposing forces have reached a virtual stalemate. The KMI policies remain in effect, and many companies have received approval to ship 56-bit DES under the government's conditions. The Security and Freedom Through Encryption (SAFE) Act never made it out of the House Commerce Committee in 1998, but a revised version has been reintroduced in 1999. This bill would lift export controls on encryption software regardless of whether that software incorporated key recovery. It affirms the rights of any U.S. citizen to use and sell encryption anywhere in the world, regardless of the bit length. The Senate's version of this is the E-Privacy Act, which also stalled in Committee in 1998. Without the passage of such legislation, the only effect of key escrow has been to delay honest users from obtaining this technology.

In September, 1999, the Clinton Administration announced a major reversal of its policy on export controls. The White House proposal would allow the export of encryption software of any length without a license. As a result, U.S. companies could export high-level encryption products to commercial firms and nongovernment users. The only requirement would be a technical review conducted by the Department of Commerce. Details of that review have not yet been disclosed.

## The Ethical Dimensions of Encryption

The heated encryption debate is closely interconnected with several of the other major themes that have been discussed in this book, specifically, privacy and free speech. According to Michael Godwin, cryptography is central to free speech on an insecure medium such as the Internet because it allows us to "speak with the assurance of confidentiality."[15]

Private citizens who are also subject to the export restriction claim that those restrictions violate their First Amendment right to free speech. The federal government, of course, denies that such restrictions violate free speech rights. Although some question whether encryption code should be considered as a form of "speech," the law seems to be siding against the federal government on this issue. In early 1997, the U.S. District Court in San Francisco ruled in favor of Daniel Bernstein, a mathematics professor, who was prohibited by the State Department from posting his encryption program on the Internet. The judge in this case determined that such a ban was an unconstitutional violation of Bernstein's free speech rights. Despite this ruling, it is unlikely that a court would strike down restrictions against encryption on behalf of commercial free speech, which is always viewed by the courts as more limited than political or academic speech.

In some respects, the government's efforts may be futile because it is virtually impossible to control cryptographic technology. At this stage, it is almost like trying to put the crypto "genie" back in the bottle. The U.S. government may just have to realize that it can no longer tightly control information flow as it did in the past. Critics of these key recovery plans often point out that high-end 128-bit encryption is widely available from non-U.S. software vendors. For example, an Australian company now sells a version of the Netscape browser with built-in 128-bit encryption. The basic problem is that international policies on encryption are inconsistent. Although some countries have a laissez-faire attitude, others, like the United States, regulate this technology through export controls. Unless there is consistency, it will be impossible to adequately control this technology.

The encryption controversy is yet another example of how technology or "code" affects and controls behavior. The purpose of encryption code is to help guarantee the privacy and security of communications. This code gives individuals the power to scramble their communication in a way that makes it difficult for law enforcement authorities or anyone else to decrypt it. Once again, however, the radically decentralized network technology is empowering the individual in a way that threatens the state. As a result, the U.S. federal government has sought to re-establish central control so that it can regulate that code in order to dictate behavior on its own terms. It is trying to limit technology through the force of law and export controls.

As we have seen, the government is afraid of *too* much privacy and confidentiality made possible by the powerful technology of encryption. Furthermore, the government's KMI proposal goes well beyond export controls because it requires certified signatures, which would authenticate the originator of an Internet transmission. Thus, although encryption technology was originally developed to enhance privacy and confidentiality, government regulation of that technology through back-door keys and certifying identities could now be used to undermine personal privacy on a large scale.

When we try to assess this issue from a moral perspective, it becomes apparent that an evaluation of consequences will be required. Moor's just consequentialism model can be helpful in analyzing this case. Recall the essentials of that model: consequentialism is constrained by the principle of justice, the protection of human rights. Justice requires impartiality, so it is unjust for anyone to adopt a policy they would not allow others to adopt.

Despite its many flaws, it is difficult to argue that the government's policy of key recovery would be regarded as unjust by all rational, impartial people. The implementation of this policy does not necessarily mean that privacy rights will be flagrantly compromised; rather by giving the government its back-door access, it opens up the *possibility* of abuse. Furthermore, unbreakable cryptography *is* a real threat to those trying to enforce the law, so there is a public safety issue at stake. On the other hand, there is nothing inherently unjust or irrational about the opposite policy that precludes key escrow and supports a strong right to electronic privacy that is willing to take some security risks to safeguard that right.

Thus, we are compelled to fall back on an objective cost/benefit analysis. Has the government made the case that the benefits of its key recovery policy exceed the costs of those plans? It appears that the single, but significant, benefit of this policy is the government's ability to exercise *limited* control over encryption: by restricting exports, there will be fewer high-end encryption systems available, and this will contribute to public safety. By keeping encryption out of countries beyond U.S. borders, the United States can conduct foreign intelligence with fewer impediments. However, there is no way these restrictions can block the use of high-end encryption software completely because they are readily available from vendors in other countries and because international policies on this technology lack consistency.

On the other hand, the costs of key recovery are high. Consider the following items:

- Higher risk that privacy rights are threatened and put into some jeopardy because the government agencies will have the key to encrypted communications

- Danger of abuse by law enforcement agencies and others who design, implement, and operate the key recovery system

- Need to build a global key recovery infrastructure (such as KMI) with high operational and transaction costs

- Risk of errors in authenticating the individual or organization requesting an archived key

- Requirement to turn over the escrowed key to foreign governments, thereby enabling some oppressive governments to decode communications of dissenters and those pressing a human rights agenda

Moreover, given that there are hundreds of encryption products, thousands of law enforcement agencies across the world, and millions of Internet users who will take advantage of encryption, the sheer scale of this project suggests that the operation of a key recovery scheme will be neither economically nor managerially viable.[16]

It would appear then that although there are undeniable benefits to key recovery, the downside of deploying this system is significant. One would be hard pressed to make the case that the benefits of this policy really outweigh these substantial costs for the community of affected stakeholders. If this is so, it follows from the vantage point of this ethical model that implementing a key recovery system in its present format would not be morally acceptable.

Is some other solution possible? Can we find any middle ground? We cannot casually ignore the problems law enforcement officials face because of encryption. So perhaps allowing a neutral international agency to have *some* control over this technology (with proper safeguards) is warranted if the world community reaches consensus on the danger of encryption in the hands of criminals. However, those safeguards must be designed with a modest infrastructure and greater respect for the privacy rights of organizations and individuals than has so far been demonstrated in U.S. public policy.

It is evident that this dilemma will not easily yield to an ideal resolution, which is why both conscientious government officials and responsible civil libertarians have grappled with this problem for many years without reaching a satisfactory compromise. Some type of key recovery mechanism may be a means of balancing competing interests if world governments find the right formula, but that is unlikely to happen. They must still try to find a way to protect their security interests without creating an Orwellian, surveillance-oriented society in order to do so.

## ▶ Securing Electronic Commerce

Hackers trespassing and defacing Web sites is just one of the risks that plague corporations and on-line vendors. Even more costly problems arise when culprits steal passwords and use phony identifiers to make fraudulent purchases. Although most e-commerce sites are secured adequately, there have been numerous security lapses, which have sometimes put sensitive consumer data at risk.

There have been alarming stories about companies rushing to build a Web site, and in their haste, downplaying the need for adequate on-line security. In other instances, inadequate technical knowledge has led to dangerous security deficiencies. In one such incident, Blarg Online, an ISP located in Seattle, reported that software products used to create the "shopping cart" feature found at many Web sites could leave credit card numbers exposed if the software was not installed correctly. The software vendors in question have fixed the problem, but this oversight is indicative of the vulnerability of customer data if on-line security is mishandled.

How can commercial Web sites be adequately secured? What are the risks of economizing on security protections? And finally what is the moral dimension of this issue—is there a moral imperative at stake here?

If vendors are to achieve a basic level of security for commercial Web sites, they must address two problems: (1) securing the Web server and the files that it contains and (2) guaranteeing the integrity of the information that travels between the Web server and the end user. This includes usernames, passwords, credit card numbers, and so forth; all of this sensitive information must be protected adequately from the risk of being intercepted by hackers or thieves.

The first challenge, then, is to secure the Web server itself. This can usually be accomplished by using standard computer security techniques, such as authentication mechanisms and intrusion protection devices. Gatekeepers and digital locks can also secure the networks on which these servers reside.

The more complicated problem is securing information in transit between the server and the user. The only sure way to secure this data is through encryption, encoding the transmitted information so that it can be read only by an authorized recipient with a proper key that decodes the information. Protocols such as the SET (Secure Electronic Transactions) standard are used to encrypt credit card information being transmitted over the Internet. An alternative protocol is Netscape's Secure Socket Layer (SSL), which automatically encrypts information sent to Web sites and then decrypts it before it is read by the recipient.

Why the need for protocols such as SSL? Consider what transpires in a typical on-line transaction. If someone decides to buy a book from an on-line book store, that person must electronically submit a credit card number along with some personal information to complete this transaction. There is a danger that the credit card number or password will be "sniffed" by hackers. Sniffers are automated programs used to seek out security lapses and to intercept vulnerable communications travelling over a network. To avoid this, SSL relies on encryption so that data travelling between the customer's Web browser and the on-line book store cannot be sniffed out or monitored while in transit. SSL also supports digital identification so that each party can verify the other's identity. This helps prevent impersonation (criminals using phony identities to purchase goods).

The best way to verify identity is through the use of *digital signatures.* This technology also relies on the use of encryption keys to encode and decode a message. In this case, a *private key* is used to sign one's signature to some message or piece of data and a *public key* is used to verify a signature after it has been sent. The public key might be published in a directory or otherwise made available to other users. Assume that John and Mary are exchanging e-mail, and Mary wants to verify John's identity. Mary can send John a letter with a random number, requesting that he digitally sign that number and send it back. John receives the letter, and digitally signs the random number with his private key. When the letter is sent back to Mary, she verifies that signature with her copy of John's public key. If the signature matches, she knows that she is communicating with John, assuming that John has been careful with his private key. These digital signatures will undoubtedly play a major role in preventing impersonation during e-commerce transactions.

According to most security analysts, fire walls must also be part of the overall security solution. A fire wall consists of hardware and/or software that are designed to insulate an organization's internal network from the Internet. Fire wall software gives access only to trusted Internet addresses and scrutinizes incoming data for irregularities or signs of danger. According to Garfinkel and Spafford, "Ideally, firewalls are configured so that all connections to an internal network go through relatively few well-monitored locations."[17] Fire walls can sometimes be used to protect the Web server, but most companies set up public Web sites outside the fire wall to make them more easily accessible to those trying to buy their products.

There are, of course, many reasons why companies should be motivated to implement these security techniques. There are certainly market pressures at work that encourage corporations to pay attention to security. Customers will punish vendors who have a cavalier attitude about their personal data and credit card numbers by shunning their Web sites. Sound security mechanisms, on the other hand, will bolster consumer confidence that the Internet is a safe place to do business.

In addition, there is a moral imperative to ensure that the level of on-line security is adequate. When customers make purchases on-line, they are placing their trust in the hands of these e-commerce companies. If those companies are negligent or lack the proper security consciousness, the result could be calamitous for customers who may find themselves as victims of credit card fraud if their credit card number is intercepted. Hence, there is a moral duty to take reasonable precautions and to implement feasible security measures that will provide for the integrity of on-line transactions and prevent harm to unsuspecting consumers. "Bad faith" efforts to secure the data of e-commerce customers cannot meet the standards of morality or the sometimes tougher standard of the marketplace.

## Discussion Questions

1. Do you agree that spam is a form of electronic trespass? If so, what are the implications for how it should be regulated?
2. Should a Web site be considered private property? In what ways should it be treated differently from physical property?
3. Where do you stand on the controversial encryption issue? Should governments like the United States be allowed to have an escrowed key to certain encrypted communications?

## CASE STUDY

### The Case of the Pretty Good Privacy Encryption Program

In June 1991, Philip Zimmerman completed a complex and elaborate encryption program, which he called *Pretty Good Privacy,* or PGP. The program is based on public key cryptography (RSA) and allows ordinary users to encrypt their messages so that they cannot be deciphered by unauthorized individuals, including law enforcement authorities. To the dismay of government officials, the program was made available free of charge to the general public. Zimmerman handed PGP over to an unidentified "friend" in the summer of 1991. That individual subsequently placed the program on a bulletin board system on the Internet for anyone to access, with no fees to pay, registration forms to fill out, or questions to answer.

Since Zimmerman has distributed this user-friendly program, it has become the most widely used encryption program in cyberspace. Zimmerman himself never shipped the product to other countries (in violation of U.S. export laws), but there is no doubt that others have taken this free program and made it available to users all over the globe. According to Zimmerman, PGP was dispersed through cyberspace "like thousands of dandelion seeds blowing in the wind."[18]

Although Zimmerman is admired by many civil libertarians and those who oppose U.S. export controls on encryption products, he does not enjoy the same status with law enforcement officials. They have contended for years that PGP interferes with their efforts to apprehend criminals and stop crime. The problem is that PGP makes it possible for terrorists or criminals to encrypt their communications, thereby making them off limits for surveillance.

According to the government's perspective, PGP has undermined U.S. export controls of encryption software and efforts to prevent uncrackable encryption programs from falling into the wrong hands. Several years ago, California police reported that PGP encryption prevented them from reading the electronic diary of a pedophile, which would have helped them crack an expanding ring of child pornographers.

Zimmerman has been investigated by the FBI and by a federal grand jury, but he has never been convicted of any wrongdoing. He has explained and justified his actions in many forums. In an essay written when PGP was just completed, he cites the need for privacy protection for all citizens as his primary motivation for writing this program:

> If privacy is outlawed, only outlaws will have privacy. Intelligence agencies have access to good cryptographic technology. So do the big arms and drug traffickers. So do defense contractors, oil companies, and other corporate giants. But ordinary people and grassroots political organizations mostly have not had access to affordable "military grade" public-key cryptographic technology. Until now.
>
> PGP empowers people to take their privacy into their own hands. There's a growing social need for it. That's why I wrote it.[19]

## Questions:

1. From a moral standpoint, do you agree with Zimmerman's decision to release PGP so freely on the Internet?
2. Are U.S. legal restrictions on programs such as PGP sound and warranted?

# References

1. Krause, J. 1998. You've been hacked.*The Industry Standard*, September 28, p. 50.
2. Yasin, R. 1998. Hackers: Users, feds vulnerable. *InternetWeek*, May 25, p.1.
3. For more background on this, see The Internet worm. In Spinello, R. A. 1995. *Ethical aspects of information technology*. Englewood Cliffs, NJ: Prentice Hall, pp. 208–212.
4. Denning, D. 1996. Concerning hackers who break into computer systems. In Ludlow, P. (Ed.). *High noon on the electronic frontier*. Cambridge, MA: MIT Press, p. 141.
5. *The Computer Fraud and Abuse Act*, Section 1030 (a), (1)–(9).
6. Spafford, E. 1992. Are computer hacker break-ins ethical? *Journal of Systems Software* January:45.
7. Johnson, D. 1994. *Computer ethics* (2nd ed). Englewood Cliffs, NJ: Prentice Hall, p. 116.
8. Hardy, T. 1996. The ancient doctrine of trespass to Web sites. *Journal of Online Law* art. 7, par. 29.
9. Ibid., par. 53.
10. *CompuServe, Inc. v. CyberPromotions, Inc.*, Case No. C2-96-1070, U.S. District Court for the Southern Division of Ohio, Eastern Division, 9624 (1015).
11. Denning, D. 1998. Encryption policy and market trends. In Denning, D. (Ed.). *Internet besieged*. Reading, MA: Addison-Wesley, p. 457.
12. Quoted in DiDio, L. 1998. Internet boosts cryptography. *Computerworld*, March 16, p. 32.
13. Barlow, J. P. 1994. Jackboots on the infobahn. *Wired* April:87.
14. Baker, S. 1994. Don't worry be happy: Why Clipper is good for you. *Wired* June:91.
15. Godwin, M. 1998. *CyberRights*. New York: Random House, p. 156.
16. A more comprehensive list of these costs is provided in an on-line White Paper by Abelson, H., et al. The risks of key recovery, key escrow, and trusted third party encryption.
17. Garfinkel, S. (with Spafford, G.). 1997. *Web security and commerce* Cambridge, MA: O'Reilly & Associates, p. 21.
18. Quoted in Levy, S. 1996. Crypto rebels. In Ludlow, P. (Ed.). *High noon on the electronic frontier*. Cambridge, MA: MIT Press, p. 192.
19. Zimmerman, P. 1996. How PGP works/why do you need PGP? In Ludlow, P. (Ed.). *High noon on the electronic frontier*. Cambridge, MA: MIT Press, p. 184.

# Glossary
## The Language
## of the Internet

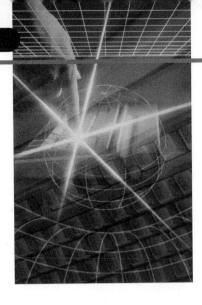

**Browser:** a software tool that enables users to navigate through the Internet and link from one Web site to another.

**Clipper Chip:** a system developed by the National Security Agency (NSA) of the United States for the encryption of telephone communications; this system was never implemented because of concerns about privacy.

**Cookie:** a small file sent to a user's browser from a Web server that often contains concise data about what that user examined at the Web site.

**Data Encryption Standard (DES):** a symmetric private key cryptography system approved by the U.S. government; the same secret binary key is used for encryption and decryption.

**Deep Linking:** the practice of linking to subordinate pages within the Web site to which one is linking instead of that site's home page (some Web sites object when their home page is bypassed).

**Digital Certificate:** provides electronic validation of the identity of someone sending a message or transmitting other data in cyberspace.

**Domain Name:** a worldwide naming convention that permits each Web site to have a unique, identifiable name.

**Eavesdropping:** electronic snooping of Internet data as it is transmitted through multiple computer systems to its final destination.

---

This is not an exhaustive list of Internet terminology, but it does provide definitions for the new and unfamiliar terms that are introduced in this book.

**E-Commerce (Electronic Commerce):** business model for generating revenues by taking advantage of the features of the World Wide Web.

**Encryption:** process whereby data is encoded or scrambled to make it unintelligible to eavesdroppers; the data is decoded or converted back to its original form by means of a key available only to the intended recipient of that data.

**Fire Wall:** security mechanism that positions hardware/software between an organization's internal computer network and the Internet.

**Framing:** occurs when a Web page author includes within that Web page material from another Web page in a "frame" or block on the screen usually with its own advertising and promotional material.

**Hypertext Markup Language (HTML):** the language used to create the text and features of a Web page.

**Internet Protocol (IP) Address:** a four-part numeric address for any system connected to the Internet so that information being transmitted over the network can be sent to its proper destination.

**Internet Service Provider (ISP):** worldwide computer networks that enable individual subscribers or organizations to link to the Internet, usually for a monthly fee.

**Linking:** a link is a connection between two different Web pages or between two different locations within the same Web page; a "hyperlink" within a Web page contains the address for another Web site, which appears in the form of an icon and is activated with the click of the mouse.

**Meta Tag:** concise description of Web pages' contents that remains invisible to the user but can be recognized by search engines.

**Open Source Code Movement:** the source code of application or operating system software is made freely available for modification, corrections, and redistribution (source code consists of a computer program's statements written in a high-level language such as JAVA or C++).

**Opt-in:** an approach to privacy based on *informed consent;* it requires vendors to seek permission before selling or reusing someone's personal information.

**Opt-out:** similar to opt-in but in this case users are notified that their personal data will be used for secondary purposes unless they disapprove and notify the vendor.

**Panoptic Sort:** term coined by Oscar Gandy that represents the use of personal data for discriminatory purposes.

**Platform for Internet Content Selection (PICS):** a labeling standard that provides a way of rating and blocking on-line material such as hate speech or pornography.

**Platform for Privacy Preferences Project (P3P):** a technological framework that relies on predefined standards set by the user to negotiate with Web sites about how that user's information will be used and disseminated to third parties.

**Portal:** Web-based interface that gives users access to multiple applications such as news services, commercial Web sites, and e-mail all through one main screen; portals also provide for search functionality.

**Pretty Good Privacy (PGP):** a method for encrypting data developed by Philip Zimmerman and made available over the Internet to interested users.

**Private Key Encryption:** encryption scheme that uses the same secret binary key to encode and decode data.

**Public Key Encryption:** one of the two keys used in the encryption process is published in a directory or otherwise made public and the other is kept private.

**RSA:** a standard public key encryption system available from RSA Data Security Inc.

**SPAM:** electronic junk mail sent in bulk form from an individual or organization promoting their goods or services to potential customers on the Internet.

**TCP/IP:** the network technology that enables data to be transferred on the Internet.

**Trusted System:** consists of hardware and/or software programmed to enforce copyright protection by enforcing usage rights that dictate how and when a digital work can be used.

**Universal Resource Locator (URL):** the unique electronic address for a Web site.

**Web Server:** the hardware system on which a Web site resides.

**World Wide Web:** a location within the Internet that provides for the multimedia presentation of information in the form of Web sites.

# Bibliography

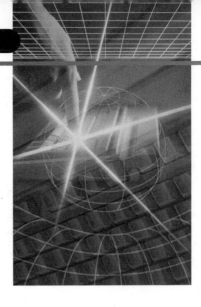

Readers are also encouraged to consult the Web site (www.jbpub.com) for additional resources.

## General Works on the Internet and Society (Chapters 1 and 2)

Doheny-Farina, S. 1996. *The wired neighborhood*. New Haven: Yale University Press.

Dyson, E. 1998. *Release 2.1*. New York: Broadway Books.

Gibson, W. 1984. *Neuromancer*. New York: Ace Books.

Grossman, W. 1997. *Net wars*. New York: New York University Press.

Hance, O. 1996. *Business and law on the Internet*. New York: McGraw-Hill.

Huber, P. 1997. *Law and disorder in cyberspace*. New York: Oxford University Press.

Kahin, B., and J. Keller (Eds.). 1995. *Public access to the Internet*. Cambridge: MIT Press.

Kahin, B., and C. Nesson (Eds.). 1997. *Borders in cyberspace: Information policy and global information infrastructure*. Cambridge: MIT Press.

Lessig, L. 1999. *Code: And other laws of cyberspace*. New York: Basic Books.

Lessig, L. "The laws of cyberspace." Paper delivered at Taiwan Net '98 Conference. http://cyber.harvard.edu/lessig.html.

Ludlow, P. (Ed.). 1996. *High noon on the electronic frontier: Conceptual issues in cyberspace*. Cambridge: MIT Press.

Miller, S. 1996. *Civilizing cyberspace: Policy, power, and the information superhighway*. Reading, MA: Addison-Wesley.

Negroponte, N. 1995. *Being digital*. New York: Knopf.

Post, D. "Of horses, black holes, and decentralized law-making in cyberspace." Paper delivered at Private Censorship/Perfect Choice conference at Yale Law School, April 9–11.

Rheingold, H. 1993. *The virtual community: Homesteading on the electronic frontier*. Reading, MA: Addison-Wesley.

Shapiro, A. 1999. *The control revolution*. New York: Century Foundation Books.

Shenk, D. 1997. *Data smog: Surviving the information glut*. New York: HarperCollins.

Stefik, M. 1996. *Internet dreams*. Cambridge, MA: MIT Press.

Stoll, C. 1995. *Silicon snake oil*. New York: Doubleday.

Wriston, W. 1992. *The twilight of sovereignty: How the information revolution is transforming our world*. New York: Charles Scribner's Sons.


## Internet and Computer Science Ethics (Chapters 1 and 2)

Baase, S. 1997. *A gift of fire: Social, legal and ethical issues in computing*. Upper Saddle River, NJ: Prentice Hall.

Bynum, T. W. 1998. *Information ethics: An introduction*. Cambridge, MA: Blackwell Publishers.

Edgar, S. 1997. *Morality and machines*. Sudbury, MA: Jones and Bartlett.

Ermann, M. D., M. Williams, and M. Shauf (Eds.). 1997. *Computers, ethics, and society*. 2nd ed. New York: Oxford University Press.

Forrester, T., and P. Morrison. 1990. *Computer ethics: Cautionary tales and ethical dilemmas in computing*. Cambridge, MA: MIT Press.

Gotterbarn, D., K. Miller, and S. Rogerson. 1997. Software engineering code of ethics. *Communications of the ACM* 40(11):110–118.

Gould, C. (Ed.). 1989. *The information web: Ethical and social implications of computers*. Boulder, CO: Westview Press.

Johnson, D. 1994. *Computer ethics*, 2nd ed. Englewood Cliffs, NJ: Prentice Hall.

Johnson, D., and H. Nissenbaum (Eds.). 1995. *Computers, ethics and social values*. Englewood Cliffs, NJ: Prentice Hall.

Kling, R. (Ed.). 1996. *Computerization and controversy*, 2nd ed. San Diego: Academic Press.

O'Reilly and Associates (Ed.). 1997. *The Internet and society* (Proceedings of Harvard Conference on the Internet and Society). Cambridge: Harvard University Press.

Rogerson, S., and T. W. Bynum. 1998. *Information ethics: A reader*. Cambridge, MA: Blackwell Publishers.

Rosenberg, R. 1997. *The social impact of computers*, 2nd ed. San Diego: Academic Press.

Severson, R. 1997. *The principles of information ethics*. Armonk, NY: M.E. Sharpe.

Spinello, R. 1995. *Ethical aspects of information technology*. Englewood Cliffs, NJ: Prentice Hall.

Spinello, R. 1997. *Case studies in information and computer ethics*. Upper Saddle River, NJ: Prentice Hall.

Willard, N. 1997. *The cyberethics reader*. New York: McGraw-Hill.


## Free Speech and Content Control (Chapter 3)

Branscomb, A. 1995. Anonymity, autonomy, and accountability: Challenges to the First Amendment in cyberspace. *Yale Law Journal* 104:1628–1645.

Elmer-Dewitt, P. 1995. Cyberporn. *Time* July 3:37–41.

Froomkin, M. 1996. Flood control on the information ocean: Living with anonymity, digital cash, and distributed data bases. *University of Pittsburgh Journal of Law and Commerce* 39:245–306.

Godwin, M. 1998. *Cyberrights*. New York: Random House.

Katz, J. 1997. *Virtuous reality*. New York: Random House.

Lessig, L. 1997. Tyranny in the infrastructure. *Wired* July:96.

Pool, I. 1983. *Technologies of freedom*. Cambridge, MA: Belknap Press.

Resnick, P., and J. Miller. 1996. PICS: Internet access controls without censorship. *Communications of the ACM* 39(10):87–93.

Rosenberg, R. 1993. Free speech, pornography, sexual harassment, and electronic networks. *The Information Society* 9:285–331.

Sopinka, J. 1997. Freedom of speech and privacy in the information age. *The Information Society* 13:171–184.

Sunstein, C. 1995. The First Amendment in cyberspace. *Yale Law Journal* 104:1757–1786.

Sunstein, C. 1993. *Democracy and the problem of free speech.* New York: Free Press.

Turner, W. B. 1996. What part of 'no law' don't you understand? A primer on the First Amendment and the Internet. *Wired* March:104–112.

Wallace, J., and M. Mangan. 1996. *Sex, laws, and cyberspace.* New York: Henry Holt Books.

## Intellectual Property (Chapter 4)

Bettig, R. 1996. *Copyrighting culture.* Boulder, CO: Westview Press.

Boyle, J. 1996. *Shamans, software and spleens.* Cambridge: Harvard University Press.

Clapes, A. L. 1993. *Softwars: The legal battles for control of the global software industry.* Westport, CT: Quorum Books.

Goldstein, P. 1994. *Copyright's highway.* New York: Hill and Wang.

Moore, A (Ed.). 1997. *Intellectual property: Moral, legal and intellectual dilemmas.* Lanham, MD: Rowman & Littlefield.

Raymond, E. 1998. The cathedral and the bazaar. www.tuxedo.org/~esr/writings/ cathedral-bazaar/cathedral.

Samuelson, P., et al. 1996. A new view of intellectual property and software, *Communications of the ACM* 39(3):21–30.

Spinello, R. 1999. Web site linking: Right or privilege. Paper Delivered at Fourth Annual Ethics and Technology Conference, Boston College.

Stallman, R. 1985. GNU manifesto. www.gnu.org/gnu/manifesto.html.

Stefik, M. 1997. Trusted systems. *Scientific American* March:78–81.

Steidlmeier, P. 1993. The moral legitimacy of intellectual property claims: American business and developing country perspectives. *Journal of Business Ethics* 16:157–164.

## Privacy Issues (Chapter 5)

Agre, P., and M. Rotenberg (Eds.). 1997. *Technology and privacy: The new landscape.* Cambridge: MIT Press.

Behar, R. 1997. Who's reading your e-mail? *Fortune* February:57–61.

Branscomb, A. 1994. *Who owns information?* New York: Basic Books.

Brin, W. 1998. *The transparent society.* Reading, MA: Addison-Wesley.

Clarke, R. 1988. Information technology and dataveillance. *Communications of the ACM* May:498–512.

DeCew, J. 1997. *In pursuit of privacy: Law, ethics, and the rise of technology.* Ithaca, NY: Cornell University Press.

Etzioni, A. 1999. *The limits of privacy.* New York: Basic Books.

Flaherty, D. 1989. *Protecting privacy in surveillance societies.* Chapel Hill, NC: University of North Carolina Press.

Gandy, O. 1993. *The panoptic sort: A political economy of personal information.* Boulder, CO: Westview Press.

Gandy, O. 1996. Coming to terms with the panoptic sort. In D. Lyon (Ed.), *Computers, surveillance & privacy.* Minneapolis: University of Minnesota Press, pp. 132–158.

Gavison, R. 1984. Privacy and the limits of the law. *Yale Law Journal* 89:421–471.

Gurak, L. 1997. *Persuasion and privacy in cyberspace.* New Haven: Yale University Press.

Lyon, D., and E. Zureik (Eds.). 1996. *Computers, surveillance, & privacy.* Minneapolis: University of Minnesota Press.

Moor, J. 1997. Towards a theory of privacy in the information age. *Computers and Society* September:27–32.

Rothfeder, J. 1992. *Privacy for sale: How computerization has made everyone's life an open secret.* New York: Simon & Schuster.

Smith, J. 1994. *Managing privacy: Information technology and corporate America.* Chapel Hill, NC: The University of North Carolina Press.

Tavani, H. 1997. Internet search engines and personal privacy. In J. van den Hoven (Ed.), *Proceedings of Conference on Computer Ethics: Philosophical Enquiry.* Rotterdam, The Netherlands: Erasmus University Press, pp. 169–178.

Ware, W. 1993. The new faces of privacy. *The Information Society* March–April:191–205.

Westin, A. 1967. *Privacy and freedom.* New York: Atheneum.

Wright, M., and J. Kahalik. 1997. The erosion of privacy. *Computers and Society* 27(4):22–26.

## Encryption and Security Issues (Chapter 6)

Barker, R. 1991. *Computer security handbook.* Blue Ridge Summit, PA: TAB Professional Reference Books.

Barlow, J. P. 1994. Jackboots on the Infobahn. *Wired* April:87–88.

Denning, D., and P. Denning. 1998. *Internet besieged.* Reading, MA: Addison-Wesley.

Diffie, W. 1998. The first ten years of public key cryptography. *Proceedings of the IEEE* May:560–577.

Froomkin, M. 1995. The metaphor is the key: Cryptography, the Clipper Chip, and the Constitution. *University of Pennsylvania Law Review* 143:709–897.

Garfinkel, S., and G. Spafford. 1997. *Web security and commerce.* New York: O'Reilly Publishing.

Hardy, I. 1996. The ancient doctrine of trespass to web sites. *Journal of Online Law,* article 7.

Hoffman, L. 1990. *Rogue programs: Viruses, worms, and Trojan horses.* New York: Van Nostrand Reinhold.

Levy, S. 1984. *Hackers.* New York: Dell Publishing.

Spafford, E. 1992. Are computer hacker break-ins ethical? *Journal of Systems Software* January:41–47.

Whitfield, D., and S. Landau. 1998. *Privacy on the line: The politics of wiretapping and encryption.* Cambridge: MIT Press.

# INDEX